Guide to Reading for Social Studies Teachers

Guide to Reading for Social Studies Teachers

Jonathon C. McLendon, Editor

Bulletin 46

NATIONAL COUNCIL FOR THE SOCIAL STUDIES

A National Affiliate of the National Education Association

1201 Sixteenth Street, N.W. Washington, D.C. 20036

$3.75

Library of Congress Catalog Card Number: 73-75298

Foreword

In the last ten years or so has come an outpouring of writing in social studies education. So much writing is heartening, but overwhelming. Educators working in a variety of fields want the best of recent scholarship and lucid, fresh presentations of ideas: teachers aiming on their own or with others to improve curriculum and instruction; curriculum workers and consultants tackling school problems; college and university educators improving their own programs, and working with pre-service and in-service teachers and others in varying professional roles; librarians mindful of what is most helpful to their patrons; and those wanting simply to know more. In a field significant for young people and society, a field full of ideas, the problem of selecting reading materials out of the enormity of what is available is difficult.

This *Guide to Reading for Social Studies Teachers* is intended to help social studies educators find their way into what they need and want to pursue. The bulletin is organized by sections and topics of the sort that social studies educators are likely to explore. Every chapter is written by a person who has studied, read extensively, and thought hard about the area he or she surveys. Their chapters citing selections are, indeed, much needed and useful guides to reading material.

The National Council for the Social Studies is deeply indebted to the editor, Jonathon McLendon, for his work on this *Guide* and for the contributions he has made to NCSS and social studies education over the years. The Council also expresses its appreciation to each of the chapter authors. All have given generously of their time, energy, and talent.

Jean Fair, *President*
National Council for the Social Studies

NATIONAL COUNCIL FOR THE SOCIAL STUDIES

The National Council for the Social Studies is a National Affiliate of the National Education Association of the United States. It is the professional organization of educators at all levels — elementary, secondary, college, and university — who are interested in the teaching of social studies. Membership in the National Council for the Social Studies includes a subscription to the Council's official journal, *Social Education,* and a copy of the Yearbook. In addition, the Council publishes bulletins, curriculum studies, pamphlets, and other materials of practical use for teachers of the social studies. Membership dues are $12.00 a year. Applications for membership and orders for the purchase of publications should be sent to the Executive Secretary, 1201 Sixteenth Street, N.W., Washington, D.C. 20036.

Introduction

The titles of more than 1300 publications recommended for social studies teachers appear in this bulletin. A great variety and number of teachers' materials were developed during the 1960's, and this made it necessary for authors of this volume to limit their comments about each cited book to a sentence or a short paragraph. Nevertheless, they have attempted to be objective, fair, and perceptive in their statements.

This bulletin aims to identify the best reading materials for social studies teachers. Space permitted the inclusion of only readings of national significance. Most local, state, regional, and individual project publications, not nationally distributed, thus are not cited. Materials for students are also omitted. Publications about general education, or other fields outside of the social studies, receive little attention. We thought it far more important to focus on areas of specific interest to social studies teachers.

The Appendix includes the names of authors whose books are cited and pages where these works are mentioned, and a directory of publishers' addresses. Such information can be valuable to readers in utilizing this bulletin.

Additional listings of bibliographies appear in several chapters; they include other references to social sciences/social studies materials. Space limitations did not permit the chapter authors to list such items as magazine articles, leaflets, stories, newspaper articles, and other related material. Most attention is given to major books and booklets of the 1960's and the beginning of the 1970's. Many publications on science, mathematics, literature, and several other fields related to social studies, both past and present, will be of value to social studies teachers, but they are too numerous to include here.

This book presents diverse sources that are available in the collections at many schools, school systems, organizations, libraries, or from publishers. Almost all publishers in social studies are listed in this bulletin. Many of these companies also produce textbooks, films, and other related student materials. Quite a number of publications are published by professional organizations. Most productive are NCSS (National Council for the Social Studies); SSEC (Social Science Education Consortium), which is growing; and several other social science and educational organizations. ERIC ChESS (Educational Resources Information Center, Clearinghouse for Social Science/Social Studies Education) identifies a growing amount of writing on specialized and general aspects of social studies. Some projects on social sciences, social studies education, and occasionally general education also produce significant social studies publications.

The authors of chapters in this bulletin are mostly outstanding leaders nationally in social studies education. Further, each of them is a specialist in the area covered by his chapter. This editor thanks each of these individuals sincerely and heartily for the contributions to this book. Their writing was especially impressive to this editor, a member of NCSS for twenty-seven years, who has not found any better group of multi-authors in any national professional publications for teachers of social studies.

It took almost four months last year to obtain the excellent services of these authors, and they required somewhere between two to six months to complete their work. Reviews of the manuscript, final editing, and printing added another seven months. As a result, as is true of any bibliographic publication, some of the material can not be completely up-to-date.

As editor of this bulletin, I want to thank several people for their assistance. A key individual in guiding the development of this publication was NCSS editor, Daniel Roselle. The advice of the NCSS Publications Board and the work of Willadene Price are also appreciated. Many hours of work, especially in typing letters, handling manuscripts, and other tasks, were contributed by our three University of Georgia Social Science Education secretaries and two student aides. My wife served as secretary, typing many preparations of this bulletin, and did the major work in arranging the contents of the Indexes.

Jonathon C. McLendon

Contents

PART THREE: Curriculum, Methods, Media

PART FOUR: Perspectives on Human Development

PART ONE

The Social Sciences

1

The Social Sciences

IRVING MORRISSETT

This chapter deals with the nature and purposes of the social sciences, taken as a whole, and with the interrelationships between two or more social sciences.

A distinction is made in this chapter between "multidisciplinary" and "interdisciplinary" relations between or among individual social sciences. "Multidisciplinary" is used to refer to parallel or consecutive presentations or uses of individual disciplines, without efforts to find common elements or to otherwise relate them closely to each other; "interdisciplinary" refers to treatments which merge or otherwise closely relate two or more disciplines to each other. There is not a sharp distinction between the two, however. Any single discipline has at least some methods and concepts common to another discipline or disciplines, while no interdisciplinary merging of a number of disciplines could prevent some parts from being clearly identifiable as belonging to particular disciplines.

The Nature and Purposes of Knowledge and of the Social Sciences

One of the most significant recent books is Leonard I. Krimerman, ed., **The Nature and Scope of Social Science: A Critical Anthology** (Appleton, 1969). This tome, weighty for its 800 pages as well as for its

---

Irving Morrissett is Executive Director, Social Science Education Consortium, Boulder, Colorado, and Professor of Economics, University of Colorado.

authors—philosophers of science, social scientists, and educators of top rank—deals with scientific method; the philosophy, nature, and methodology of the social sciences; and values and objectivity in the social sciences. A brief treatment of the same topics can be found in Chapters 1-5 and 16-17 of Peter R. Senn, **Social Science and Its Methods** (Holbrook, 1971, pb) and in Chapters 1 and 11 of Norman MacKenzie, **A Guide to the Social Sciences** (New America Library, 1966; Mentor, 1968, pb).

While the readings cited in this book are generally confined to publications of the last decade or so, a few classics published earlier will occasionally be cited. In the present context, a deserving reference is Charles A. Beard, **The Nature of the Social Sciences** (Scribner's, 1934), particularly Chapter 1, on the nature of the social sciences, and Chapters 7-10, on uses of the social sciences in the curriculum.

The nature of knowledge, and of social science as a part of the general body of knowledge, is dealt with insightfully in Philip H. Phenix, **Realms of Meaning** (McGraw, 1964). The nature of disciplines and their role in education and the curriculum, although not specifically the social sciences, is illuminated by Arthur R. King, Jr., and John A. Brownell, **The Curriculum and the Disciplines of Knowledge** (Wiley, 1966), especially in Chapter 3, which describes ten functions and aspects of disciplines.

Briefer and simpler presentations of the nature and purposes of the social sciences are often found in social studies methods texts. Jonathon C. McLendon, **Social Studies in Secondary Education** (Macmillan, 1965), devotes Chapters 4 and 7 to this purpose, while Bruce R. Joyce, **New Strategies for Social Education** (SRA, 1972), devotes almost a third of its pages to the nature and uses of the social sciences. Both texts include useful chapter-end references.

Methodology of the Social Sciences

Main Trends of Research in the Social and Human Sciences; Part 1: Social Sciences (UNESCO, 1970), while predominantly a weighty review of research, contains two lengthy chapters by Jean Piaget which can serve other purposes. Chapter 1, "The Place of the Sciences of Man in the System of Sciences," supplements the references given in the preceding section. Chapter 7, "General Problems of Interdisciplinary Research and Common Mechanisms," gives a great deal of insight into the methodology of the social sciences. Maurice Duverger, **An Introduction to the Social Sciences, with Special Reference to Their Methods** (Praeger, 1964) examines in depth a number of selected techniques used in the social sciences.

The definitive work on methodology is Abraham Kaplan, **The Conduct of Inquiry: Methodology for Behavioral Science** (Chandler, 1964).

Difficult but extremely rewarding to read, this book covers all of the major concepts and methods of scientific endeavor, applying each of them specifically to the behavioral sciences.

The Structure of Knowledge and of the Social Sciences

Efforts during the last decade to select and present the essential elements and relationships of particular fields of knowledge for use in curriculum materials have led to construction of various "structures" of knowledge or of particular disciplines. Ideas about the nature of structure, as well as particular structures of the social sciences, are contained in G. Wesley Sowards, **The Social Studies: Curriculum Proposals for the Future** (Scott, Foresman, 1963, pb); G. W. Ford and Lawrence Pugno, **The Structures of Knowledge and the Curriculum** (Rand McNally, 1964, pb); Irving Morrissett, ed., **Concepts and Structure in the New Social Science Curricula** (Holt, 1967, pb); William T. Lowe, **Structure and the Social Studies** (Cornell University Press, 1969); and a series of papers published by the Social Science Education Consortium in 1966: Robert Perrucci, **Sociology;** Peter Greco, **The Structure of Geography;** David Collier, **The Political System;** Lawrence Senesh, **Economics;** and Paul Bohannan, **Anthropology.**

Multidisciplinary Social Science

A number of editors, authors, and groups of authors have offered presentations of the content of many or all of the social sciences in a single book or in a series of publications. These include Bernard Berelson, ed., **The Behavioral Sciences Today** (Basic Books, 1963); Norman MacKenzie, ed., **A Guide to the Social Sciences** (New American Library, 1966; Mentor, 1968, pb), Chapters 2-9; Martin Feldman and Eli Seifman, eds., **The Social Studies: Structures, Models, and Strategies** (Prentice-Hall, 1969, pb); John U. Michaelis and A. Montgomery Johnston, eds., **The Social Sciences, Foundations of the Social Studies** (Allyn and Bacon, 1965, pb); the Charles E. Merrill Social Science Seminar Series, a group of six paperbacks edited by Raymond H. Muessig and Vincent R. Rogers (1965); and Bert F. Hoselitz, ed., **A Reader's Guide to the Social Sciences** (Free Press, 1970). The most comprehensive coverage is in the Behavioral and Social Sciences Surveys (known as **"BASS"**) of each of the social sciences. These were sponsored by the National Academy of Sciences and the Social Science Research Council and published in separate volumes in 1969 and 1970 by Prentice-Hall. Edited by a number of experts in the subject areas, they cover the nature of each discipline, as well as its methods, research, and uses in public and private affairs. A summary volume, **Outlook and Needs,** gives recommendations for improving both the results and the usefulness of the social sciences.

Interdisciplinary Social Science

"Interdisciplinary" has been defined above as the merging or relating of two or more disciplines. There are many ways in which the merging or relating may take place.

In Muzafer Sherif and Carolyn W. Sherif, eds., **Interdisciplinary Relationships in the Social Sciences** (Aldine, 1969), most of the authors belie the title by sticking very close to the individual disciplines they know best. However, Chapters 1, 5, and 19 give some promising ideas about how social scientists can move toward more interdisciplinary work. Donald T. Campbell performs a particularly useful function in Chapter 19 by arguing persuasively that the interdisciplinary scientist does not have to fit the model of a twentieth-century Renaissance Man.

Bernard Berelson and Gary A. Steiner, in **Human Behavior: An Inventory of Scientific Findings** (Harcourt, 1964), describe 1,045 findings of research — a unique undertaking that has made this work a classic. The book qualifies as interdisciplinary because the findings are organized by categories that cut across disciplines, such as methods of inquiry, organizations, and institutions. The authors define "behavioral science" as "the disciplines of anthropology, psychology, and sociology — *minus* . . . physiological psychology, archaeology, technical linguistics, and most of physical anthropology; *plus* social geography, some psychiatry, and the behavioral parts of economics, political science, and law." They thus contradict Kenneth Boulding, who says in a book cited below that the term "behavioral science" is a synonym for social science, coined because some congressmen think social science has something to do with socialism.

Irving Morrissett and W. Williams Stevens, Jr., eds., present, in **Social Science in the Schools: A Search for Rationale** (Holt, 1971), the content and curricular uses of a number of individual social sciences. In addition, they illustrate three approaches to interdisciplinary work, through chapters contributed by Lawrence Senesh, Alfred Kuhn, and Kenneth Boulding.

Senesh's approach is to "orchestrate" the various social sciences in problem-solving situations, using each social science as it is most appropriate in analyzing and solving a social problem. Other interdisciplinary uses of social sciences in problem solving are illustrated in Peter R. Senn, **Social Science and Its Methods** (Holbrook, 1970, pb), Chapters 12-15, and Donald W. Calhoun, **Social Science in an Age of Change** (Harper, 1971).

Alfred Kuhn's approach to interdisciplinary social science is to identify powerful concepts and relationships that are common to two or more disciplines and to build an interdisciplinary structure on these. In his great work, **The Study of Society: A Unified Approach** (Irwin, 1963), he uses concepts and relationships such as cybernetic systems, communications, decisions, transactions, and organizations. Somewhat similar to Kuhn's approach is the work of others who have found commonalities among the social sciences, such as commonality of explanations in Robert Brown, **Explanation in Social Science** (Aldine, 1963, pb), and commonality of concepts in Barry K. Beyer and Anthony N. Penna, **Concepts in the Social Studies** (NCSS, 1971, pb) and in Charles Jung, Ronald Lippitt, Robert Fox, and Mark Chesler, **Retrieving Social Science Knowledge for Secondary Curriculum Development** (SSEC, 1966, pb).

Among those few social scientists who have worked to advance the theoretical and conceptual structure of interdisciplinary social science, Kenneth Boulding has probably made the most, and the most varied, contributions. He has analyzed the shortcomings of the social sciences and suggested some of the intellectual tools needed to bring them together in **The Impact of the Social Sciences** (Rutgers University Press, 1966); used his own discipline of economics as a base on which to build relationships with other social sciences in **Economics as a Science** (McGraw, 1970) and **Beyond Economics: Essays on Society, Religion, and Economics** (U. of Mich. Press, 1968); and invented powerful new conceptual tools and systems for analyzing social systems and social problems in **A Primer on Social Dynamics: History as Dialectics and Development** (Free Press, 1970, pb) and **Conflict and Defense: A General Theory** (Harper, 1962).

Bibliographic Sources

Many of the references cited above contain useful citations for further reading. Additional general references are Carl M. White and Associates, **Sources of Information in the Social Sciences** (The Bedminster Press, 1964); Peter R. Senn and Mary Senn, **A Short Guide to the Literature of the Social Sciences** (SSEC, 1968, pb); Julius Gould and William L. Kolb, **A Dictionary of the Social Sciences** (Free Press, 1964); and David L. Sills, ed., **International Encyclopedia of the Social Sciences** (17 volumes, Macmillan and Free Press, 1968). While the latter reference is a competent updating of **Encyclopedia of the Social Sciences** (15 volumes, Macmillan, 1930-35), the older work is still useful for its treatment of topics up to its date of publication.

2

Anthropology

WILFRID C. BAILEY

Until recently anthropology has not been treated as a separate subject matter and there has been only limited materials available for classroom use. However, anthropological information has been used for many years as a part of a variety of units and especially in units on history and on American Indians.

While physical anthropology studies the biological nature of man, anthropology includes archaeology (the study of cultures of the past), ethnology (the comparative study of particular tribal groups), social anthropology (the analysis of society and culture), and linguistics (the study of language). The unifying theme of cultural anthropology is the understanding of the development and functioning of culture, while physical anthropologists are concerned with the development of man and his capacity for culture. Anthropology studies man in both time and space. This discussion of literature is limited to cultural anthropology.

An Introduction to Anthropology

Several brief and easily understood books were written to give the basis of anthropology. An early but still useful prize winner is Clyde Kluckhohn's **Mirror For Man: The Relation of Anthropology to Modern Life** (McGraw-Hill, 1949, pb). This book had its seventeenth printing in

---

Wilfrid C. Bailey is Professor of Anthropology, Department of Anthropology, University of Georgia, Athens, Georgia.

1971. Douglas L. Oliver wrote a more recent volume, **Invitation to Anthropology** (Natural History, 1964, pb). Pertti J. Pelto wrote **The Study of Anthropology** (Merrill, 1965, pb) especially for teachers. This edition has a concluding chapter suggesting methods for school teachers. **Anthropology** (Prentice-Hall, 1970, pb), edited by Allan H. Smith and John L. Fischer, contains chapters on anthropology as a profession. Walter Goldschmidt prepared a pamphlet for students considering going into anthropology, **On Becoming an Anthropologist. A Career Pamphlet for Students** (American Anthropological Assn., 1970, pb). The last two are a must for teachers in a position to offer counsel to students who become interested in anthropology as a career. For more detail, the teacher could consult any of the standard introductory textbooks such as Lowell D. Holmes, **Anthropology: An Introduction** (Ronald, 1971); E. Adamson Hoebel, **Anthropology: The Study of Man** (McGraw-Hill, 1972); Ralph L. Beals and Harry Hoijer, **An Introduction to Anthropology** (Macmillan, 1971); or Marvin Harris, **Culture, Man, and Nature: An Introduction to General Anthropology** (Crowell, 1971).

Two brief works that deal with the general nature of culture include Ernest L. Schusky and T. Patrick Culbert, **Introducing Culture** (Prentice-Hall, 1963, pb). With a preface by Margaret Mead, a widely-known book by Ruth Benedict, **Patterns of Culture** (Houghton Mifflin, 1959, pb), describes primitive society, various cultures, and other aspects of anthropology.

Archaeology

Archaeology is probably the most popular and best known field of anthropology. There is hardly an area of the United States that does not have archaeological sites or ruins. Three books on the general nature of archaeology are listed here. Maurice Robbins and Mary B. Irving, **The Amateur Archaeologist's Handbook** (Crowell, 1965) provides not only a good introduction for the non-specialist but contains useful appendices that would be of help in obtaining local and regional information. A briefer and somewhat more technical book on method is James Deetz, **Invitation to Archaeology** (Natural History, 1967, pb). Frank Hole and Robert F. Heizer, **An Introduction to Prehistory Archaeology** (Holt, 1969) provides a more thorough account of how archaeologists work.

An attractive book on world prehistory is Clement W. Meighan's **Archaeology: An Introduction** (Chandler, 1966, pb). Chester S. Chard, **Man in Prehistory** (McGraw-Hill, 1968) provides a somewhat more detailed account of the development of cultures around the world. Old World prehistory has popularity that ties in with many history courses. Brief introductions are Grahame Clark, **The Stone Age Hunters** (McGraw-Hill, 1968, pb) and Robert J. Braidwood, **Prehistoric Men** (Scott, Foresman, 1967, pb). Grahame Clark and Stuart Piggott, **Prehistoric**

Societies (Knopf, 1965) covers the period up to the dawn of written history. A more detailed account covering both prehistory and the early civilization in the Old World can be found in Jacquetta Hawkes, **Prehistory** (Mentor, 1965, pb) and Leonard Woolley, **The Beginnings of Civilization** (Mentor, 1965, pb). They originally appeared in a combined one-volume hardback (Harper & Row, 1962).

A brief overview of the cultural history of the New World is to be found in William T. Sanders and Joseph Marino, **New World Prehistory,** (Prentice-Hall, 1970, pb). An account with original narratives was compiled by Leo Deuel, **Conquistadors Without Swords** (St. Martin's & Macmillan, 1967, pb). A lively book with much of the historical lore of American archaeology is Louis A. Brennan, **American Dawn: A New Model of American Prehistory** (Macmillan, 1971). Two rather detailed outlines of North American prehistory are to be found in Jesse D. Jennings, **Prehistory of North America** (McGraw-Hill, 1970) and Gordon R. Willey, **An Introduction to American Archaeology: North and Middle America; South America** (Prentice-Hall, 1966, 1971). Two regional coverages of Latin America are Wendell C. Bennett and Junius B. Bird, **Andean Culture History: The Archaeology of the Central Andes from Early Man to the Inca** (Natural History, 1964, pb), and William T. Sanders and Barbara J. Price, **Mesoamerica: The Evolution of Civilization** (Random House, 1968, pb).

Ethnology and Social Anthropology

Although it is possible to make distinctions between enthnology and social anthropology, the nonspecialist will see very little difference in the literature. Some people combine these two fields under the label of cultural anthropology. Much of the study of cultures around the world requires living with the people. Two edited collections contain personal accounts of anthropologists in the field. They are George D. Spindler, ed., **Being an Anthropologist: Fieldwork in Eleven Cultures** (Holt, 1970, pb), and Morris Freilich, ed., **Marginal Natives: Anthropologists at Work** (Harper & Row, 1970). Literature on specific world culture areas and tribes is too massive to adequately review here. Two types of materials are available to the teacher. First are those written by anthropologists. Of special interest to teachers who want short, interesting accounts is an extensive paperback series published by Holt, and edited by George Spindler. Approximately 50 of the books cover most of the world and a wide variety of cultures. They range from C.W.M. Hart and Arnold R. Pilling, **The Tiwi of North Australia** (1960), through William Bascom, **The Yoruba of Southwestern Nigeria** (1969), to R. Lincoln Keiser, **The Vice Lords: Warriors of the Streets** (1969), an account of Black ghetto culture. Another type of literature, written by authors on children's books, is extremely well done. For example, Sonia

Bleeker's long series includes **The Masai Herders of East Africa,** and **The Sioux Indians: Hunters and Warriors of the Plains** (Morrow, 1963, 1962, pb).

Linguistics

Anthropological linguistics developed out of the study of non-western European languages. Although there are departments of linguistics, the subject has always been important to anthropology. For a brief not-too-technical work, see Joseph H. Greenberg, **Anthropological Linguistics: An Introduction** (Random House, 1968, pb). A somewhat more detailed introduction to linguistics can be found in Ronald W. Langacker's, **Language and Its Structure: Some Fundamental Linguistic Concepts** (Harcourt, 1968, pb), and Robert A. Hall, Jr., **Introductory Linguistics** (Chilton, 1964). Teachers who work with ethnic groups will find many of the articles in a collection edited by Frederick Williams, **Language and Poverty** (Markham, 1970), both helpful and interesting.

Applied Anthropology

Anthropological knowledge of world cultures has been put to use in many ways. George M. Foster's interesting little book, **Applied Anthropology** (Little, Brown, 1969), discusses the nature of applied anthropology. Conrad M. Arensberg and Arthur H. Niehoff in **Introducing Social Change: A Manual for Community Development** (Aldine-Atherton, 1971, pb) have provided description of the use of anthropology in developmental programs. For edited collections of essays on introduced change in various parts of the world, read Arthur H. Niehoff's, **A Casebook of Social Change** (Aldine, 1966, pb), and James A. Clifton, **Applied Anthropology: Readings in the Uses of the Science of Man** (Houghton Mifflin, 1970, pb).

Anthropology of Education

A rapidly developing aspect of social anthropology is the anthropology of education which studies the process through which culture is transmitted from generation to generation. This includes schools as a cultural institution. Edited collections of articles that illustrate the dimensions of the anthropology of education include George Spindler, **Education and Culture: Anthropological Approaches** (Holt, 1965, pb); John H. Chilcott, Norman C. Greenberg, and Herbert B. Wilson, **Readings in the Socio-Cultural Foundation of Education** (Wadsworth, 1967, pb); and Harry M. Lindquest, **Education: Readings in the Process of Cultural Transmission** (Houghton Mifflin, 1970, pb). For a description of an experimental teacher program pairing anthropology and education, see Ruth Landes, **Culture in American Education: Anthropological Approaches to Minority and Dominant Groups in the Schools** (Wiley, 1965). Theodore Brameld used anthropological methods in **Japan: Culture, Education and Change in Two Communities** (Holt, 1968). A series of publications that will be of great interest to teachers is the **Case Studies in Education and Culture** edited by George and Louise Spindler. The most recent of these is John A. Hostetler and Gertrude Enders Huntington, **Children in Amish Society: Socialization and Community Education** (Holt, 1971, pb).

Teaching Materials in Anthropology

Although anthropological literature is extensive and teachers have been utilizing anthropological concepts and data in the classroom, there has been only a limited amount of material written specially for classroom use. Two projects of the 1960's produced teaching units. The Anthropology Curriculum Study Project of the American Anthropological Association has worked at the high school level. It developed a semester course, **Patterns in Human History** (Macmillan, 1971), accompanied by a variety of teaching aids. This same project also produced James J. Gallagher, **An Annotated Bibliography of Anthropological Materials for High School Use** (Macmillan, 1967, pb). The Anthropology Curriculum Project, located at the University of Georgia, prepared units for lower grades, kindergarten into secondary school level. These units include "Concept of Culture," "Development of Man and His Culture," "Culture Change," "Life Cycle," "Language," and "Race, Caste and Prejudice." The teachers' background materials for these units are useful aids for teaching at any grade level.

More traditional textbooks written for high school use, listed in order of increasing difficulty, are Stanley A. Freed and Ruth S. Freed, **Man from the Beginning** (Creative Educational Society, 1967); Lois Brauer Cover, **Anthropology for Our Times** (Oxford Univ., 1971); and Zdenek Salzmann, **Anthropology** (Harcourt, 1969). High school and junior college teachers will find helpful suggestions in two volumes edited by David G. Mandlebaumn, Gabriel W. Lasker, and Ethel M. Albert, **The Teaching of Anthropology** and **Resources for the Teaching of Anthropology** (American Anthropological Assn., both 1963, pb). One section contains "A Basic List of Books and Periodicals for College Libraries" by Rexford Beckham which has become a standard list from which to build library holdings.

3

Economics

GEORGE G. DAWSON

Economics is a vitally important subject. Much of the major legislation considered by law-making bodies at all levels is economic in nature, and most current problems have economic dimensions. All social studies subjects contain a certain amount of economics, and a knowledge of its basic principles will add greatly to one's understanding of many key events and issues in these fields. Unfortunately, many teachers manage to evade a formal study of economics during their college years, and thus they have difficulty in coping with the economic content of the curriculum. This chapter suggests a number of books that will help the teacher to learn basic economics or to review, update, and strengthen past learnings.

An Easy Introduction to Economics

Several brief, readable, and simple books are available to give the teacher an idea of what economics is all about. Among these are M. A. Robinson, Morton and Calderwood, **An Introduction to Economic Reasoning** (Brookings, 1967, pb), John Maher, **What Is Economics?** (Wiley, 1969, pb), and Albert Alexander, **The Challenge of Economics** (Pitman, 1970). Works on economics which also contain material on teaching are R. S. Martin and Miller, **Economics and Its Significance** and Russell McLaughlin, **Economics and Education** (both Merrill, 1965, 1968,

---

George G. Dawson is Director of Research and Publications and Managing Editor of *The Journal of Economic Education,* Joint Council on Economic Education, New York, New York.

pb). **Economics in the Curriculum** by J. D. Calderwood, Lawrence and Maher (Wiley, 1970, pb) suggests the grade placement of important concepts. The relationship of economics to important current issues is the focus of Ralph Kaminsky, ed., **Introduction to Economic Issues** (Doubleday, 1970, pb), Robert Heilbroner and Arthur Ford, **Is Economics Relevant?** (Goodyear, 1971, pb) and Robert Carson, **The American Economy in Conflict** (Heath, 1971). E. J. Mishan's **21 Popular Economic Fallacies** (Praeger, 1970) and Don Paarlberg's **Great Myths of Economics** (New American Library, 1968) will help clarify many basic concepts.

The Details of Basic Economics

Once the teacher has introduced himself to economics through such works, he should tackle the more detailed expositions. Any standard text used in college principles of economics courses will be useful. Among the better known are Paul Samuelson's **Economics** (McGraw-Hill, 1970) and G. L. Bach's **Economics: An Introduction to Analysis and Policy** (Prentice-Hall, 1971). Somewhat simpler are R. L. Heilbroner's **The Economic Problem** (Prentice-Hall, 1970) and W. Carl Biven's **An Introduction to Economics** (Merrill, 1970). Those who favor programmed texts might use Lloyd Reynolds, **Principles of Economics** (Learning Systems, 1971, pb).

Economics is usually divided into *macroeconomics,* which deals with aggregates (such as the nation's total output, employment, or savings) and *microeconomics,* which deals with parts of the economy (such as the actions of individuals or business firms). Most basic texts include both, but several concentrate on only one. Those interested primarily in macro might read Willis Peterson's **Principles of Economics: Macro** (Irwin, 1971, pb), Frederick S. Brooman and Henry D. Jacoby, **Macroeconomics** (Aldine, 1970), or R. E. Attiyeh, K. Lumsden and Bach, **Macroeconomics: A Programmed Book** (Prentice-Hall, 1970, pb). In each of these cases there are companion works on microeconomics (same publishers and dates).

Special Areas of Economics

All social studies subjects include some economics, and the teacher should be aware of this in order to do a thorough job of teaching them. For government's role, see Emmette Redford's **American Government and the Economy** (Macmillan, 1965) or H. H. Liebhafsky, **American Government and Business** (Wiley, 1971). John Alexander's **Economic Geography** (Prentice-Hall, 1963) or **The Geography of Economic Activity** by R. S. Thoman, Conkling and Yeates (McGraw-Hill, 1968) will help relate economics to geography. Also see these same-titled books by

G. C. Fite and Reese (Houghton Mifflin, 1965) and F. W. Tuttle and Perry (South-Western, 1970), **An Economic History of the United States.** For a shorter work, see Harvey Bunke, **A Primer on United States Economic History** (Random House, 1969, pb). Heilbroner's **The Making of Economic Society** (Prentice-Hall, 1970, pb) briefly surveys economic history from ancient Egypt to the present. Another short work is Paul Hohenberg's **A Primer on the Economic History of Europe** (Random House, 1969, pb).

Many teachers become interested in one or a few topics. Indeed, in some high schools economics is taught by teams in which each teacher specializes in certain topics. Labor's role is set forth in D. C. Bok and Dunlop, **Labor and the American Community** (Simon & Schuster, 1970, pb) and Abraham Gitlow, **Labor and Manpower Economics** (Irwin, 1971). For a perspective on business, see Harry Trebing, ed., **The Corporation in the American Economy** (Quadrangle, 1970, pb), Willard Mueller, **A Primer on Monopoly and Competition** (Random House, 1969, pb), or Richard Barber, **The American Corporation** (Dutton, 1970). Consumer problems are dealt with in Marguerite Burk's **Consumption Economics** (Wiley, 1968), L. J. Gordon and Lee, **Economics for Consumers** (American Book, 1967), and briefly in Elizabeth Gilboy's **A Primer on the Economics of Consumption** (Random House, 1968, pb). Because of the many popular fallacies surrounding money and banking, teachers should improve their knowledge through such works as George Sause, **Money, Banking and Economic Activity** (Heath, 1966), William Dunkman, **Money, Credit, and Banking** (Random House, 1969) or Peter Bernstein's **A Primer on Money, Banking, and Gold** (Random House, 1965, pb). International economic issues are also frequently misunderstood. For clarification, see James Ingram's **International Economic Problems** (Wiley, 1970, pb), Sidney Wells, **International Economics** (Atherton, 1969), or Jan Pen, **A Primer on International Trade** (Random House, 1967, pb).

It is essential to relate economic theory to current problems. Business fluctuations, poverty, agriculture, conservation, and urban issues will be receiving attention for years to come. The ups and downs of the economy are treated in Arthur Burns, **The Business Cycle in a Changing World** (Columbia Univ., 1970) and Maurice Lee, **Fluctuations, Growth, and Stability** (Irwin, 1970). The plight of the poor is discussed in R. E. Will and H. G. Vatter, eds., **Poverty in Affluence** (Harcourt, 1970, pb), David Hamilton, **A Primer on the Economics of Poverty** (Random House, 1968, pb), and Joseph Kershaw, **Government Against Poverty** (Brookings, 1970, pb). For the farm situation, consult Earl Heady's **A Primer on Food, Agriculture, and Public Policy** (Random House, 1967, pb), or Margaret Capstick's **The Economics of Agriculture** (St. Martin's, 1970). Many basic concepts are related to farming in **Economics: Applications to Agriculture and Agribusiness** by E. P. Roy, Corty and Sullivan (Interstate, 1971).

Among the many works on natural resources, environment, and pollution is **Environmental Economics** by Thos. D. Crocker and A. G. Rogers (Dryden, 1971). Problems of urban areas are explored in David Gordon's **Problems in Political Economy and Urban Perspective** (Heath, 1970) and Dick Netzer's **Economics and Urban Problems** (Basic Books, 1970). Population and economic development are vital topics. For vital aspects, refer to S. Schiavo-Campo and H. Singer, **Perspectives of Economic Development** (Houghton Mifflin, 1970) and John Pincus, ed., **Reshaping the World Economy: Rich Countries and Poor** (Prentice-Hall, 1968, pb).

To understand other economic systems, the teacher might study George Halm's **Economic Systems** (Holt, 1968) or M. T. Schnitzer and James Nordyke, **Comparative Economic Systems** (South-Western, 1971). Ideas of the great economists are explained in Charles Cole's **The Economic Fabric of Society** (Harcourt, 1969, pb), Heilbroner's **The Worldly Philosophers** (Simon & Schuster, 1967, pb), and Richard Gill's **Evolution of Modern Economics** (Prentice-Hall, 1967, pb).

Teaching Economics

For practical advice on how to teach economics there are several publications of special value. A relatively short book clearly serves as a textbook for teachers: Edward Prehn's **Teaching High School Economics** (Pitman, 1968). Other materials for teachers have been developed by specific organizations. Outstanding works, for teachers from the elementary through the college level, include numerous publications of the Joint Council on Economic Education (JCEE). Supported by the Kazanjian Foundation, the activities of the Joint Council are evident in the Foundation's annual report titled **Economic Education Experiences of Enterprising Teachers** (pb). Another productive organization is the Committee for Economic Development (CED). Some booklets for teachers on **Teaching Economics in Elementary Schools,** involving middle and upper grades instruction, are produced by the Industrial Relations Center (Univ. of Chicago, 1971, pb). Analogous material for teachers at higher grade levels is available from Purdue University and SSEC/ERIC ChESS.

4

Human Geography

CLYDE F. KOHN

Contemporary publications in human geography reflect two quite opposing approaches to research and teaching in the discipline. Until recently most geographers have maintained that their discipline was a study of unique places or things. In their research and teaching, they assumed and used laws to gain understandings of the nature and distribution of particular places or phenomena, but they did not consider it their task to discover such laws. A growing number of modern geographers, on the other hand, have begun to view their discipline as being nomothetic, that is, designed to lead towards hypotheses, laws, and theories. The first school of geographers has produced through the years a large number of valuable descriptions and interpretations of particular places or areas (descriptive regional geography), and studies of the nature and distribution of similar kinds of natural or cultural phenomena (descriptive topical or systematic geography). Those who have adopted the nomothetic approach in their research have become interested in at least three major problem areas: locational theory, human ecology (man and environment), and the spatial aspects of human behavior. This review of important recently published books will be directed, therefore, to six types of studies, involving both the descriptive and the more scientific schools of thought—regional, descriptive systematic, location theory, behavioral, ecological, and methodological.

Clyde F. Kohn is Chairman, Department of Geography, University of Iowa, Iowa City, Iowa.

Regional Studies

A number of recent geographical studies of significant areas are both intellectually stimulating and analytically rewarding. Unfortunately, space does not permit the listing of all of them. Representative of this group is Norman J. G. Pounds' **Geographical Analysis of Eastern Europe** (Longman, 1969). The first part of this book offers a summary treatment of the eight countries between the Soviet Union and the now-permeable iron curtain. The second part consists of detailed regional surveys of the individual countries and their subregions. D. W. Meinig's **Imperial Texas: An Interpretive Essay in Cultural Geography** (Univ. of Texas, 1969) provides an examination of Texas as a culture, a region, and an empire fused in the consciousness of a people and expressed in their perception, symbolization, and organization of space. A well-written book dealing with a smaller region is **St. Croix Border Country** by Harry Swain and Cotton Mather (Trimbelle, 1968). This book describes the outer edge of a growing metropolis, emphasizing the major geographic processes at work in such an area. Other regional books of special note include Donald W. Fryer's **Emerging Southeast Asia: A Study in Growth and Stagnation** (McGraw-Hill, 1970). This text deals with the complex interactions between nature and societies, between culture and economy, and between political ideologies and the organization of area. **Canada: A Geographical Interpretation,** edited by John Warkentin (Methuen, 1968) is an excellent book, and should be read by anyone who is interested in, or who teaches about, Canada. And, as a final representative of the regional school of thought, attention should be called to the book, **West Africa,** by W. B. Morgan and J. C. Pugh (Barnes & Noble, 1969), a very readable, informative, and instructive volume.

Descriptive Systematic Studies

During the 1960's, a number of books dealing with the distribution of economic, political, and social phenomena were published. Among these, in economic geography, are J. E. Spencer's book, **Shifting Cultivation in Southeastern Asia** (Univ. of California, 1966, pb); **A Preface to Economic Geography,** by Harold H. McCarty and James B. Lindberg (Prentice-Hall, 1966); **Readings in Economic Geography,** edited by Robert H. T. Smith, Edward J. Taaffe, and Leslie J. King (Rand McNally, 1968, pb); **The Economics of African Development,** by Andrew M. Marack (Praeger, 1967), although not a geography book *per se,* is nonetheless of great geographical value; **Soviet and East European Agriculture** by Jerzy F. Karcz (Univ. of California, 1967); **Basic Industrial Resources of the U. S. S. R.,** by Theodore Shabad (Columbia Univ., 1969); and **Locational Factors and Locational Developments in the Soviet Chemical Industry,** an excellent, methodical and readable presentation of this topic by Leslie Djenes, Research Paper No. 119, Department of Geography, (Univ. of Chicago, 1969). Many others could also be recommended.

Important recent contributions to political and social geography include Glenn T. Trewartha's **A Geography of Population: World Patterns** (Wiley, 1969, pb); **Geography of Religions** by David E. Sopher (Prentice-Hall, 1967, pb); and **A Geography of Mankind** by Jan O. M. Broek and John W. Webb (McGraw-Hill, 1968). **The Structure of Political Geography,** edited by Roger E. Kasperson and Julian V. Minghi (Aldine, 1969), also demonstrates the usefulness of the behavioralist orientation in geography.

Studies in Location Theory

Studies in location theory identify abstract spatial concepts and principles, and commonly test these with emphasis upon the interaction of economic, urban, and transportation phenomena in regional systems. These studies, unlike the descriptive systematic studies referred to in the preceding section, represent the new approach in geography, that is, the development of laws and theories. Among recent publications in this area of geographic specialization is Peter Haggett's **Locational Analysis in Human Geography** (St. Martin's, 1966). This book discusses the geographically significant aspects of a number of theoretical models. Another representative of this new approach is **Geographic Perspectives on Urban Systems: With Integrated Readings,** prepared by Brian J. L. Berry and Frank B. Horton (Prentice-Hall, 1970). Because scholars trained in the nomothetic approach to locational analysis are only beginning to publish substantive materials, relatively few books are yet on the market. Others are anticipated in the near future.

Behavioral Studies

Working within a pattern emphasizing process, research in geography has expanded in several new directions during the past decade. A growing number of young scholars are becoming interested, for example, in describing and understanding the spatial aspects of social, economic, and political behavior of individuals or aggregates of individuals having similar attributes. The behavioral approach can be seen as being quite different from that which emphasizes the character of a particular region and the way it differs from other regions. The emphasis is more on the spatial dynamics and processes of human behavior instead of the form and structure of particular places. The materials developed by the High School Geography Project reflect this philosophy.

Among the first to publish in this area was Allan Pred. He has written **Behavior and Location: Foundations for a Geographic Dynamic Location Theory, Part 1,** and **Behavior and Location, Part II: Lund Studies in Geography,** No. 27 and 28 (Royal Univ. of Lund, Sweden, 1967 and 1969). Richard Morrill's **The Spatial Organization of Society** (Wadsworth, 1970) contains the broad outlines of a theory of spatial organization and behavior, and a presentation of current research within this general structure. **Strategies of American Water Management** by Gilbert F. White (Univ. of Michigan, 1969) visualizes American water management policy as a series of strategies, where a strategy is defined as a combination of aims, means, and decision criteria.

Of special importance in recent years have been the publications dealing with communication processes which underlie current theories of spatial diffusion and migration. The monograph by Lawrence Brown, **Diffusion Dynamics,** No. 29, Lund Studies in Geography, (Univ. of Lund, Lund, Sweden, 1968) is especially noteworthy, although quite academic in its approach.

The danger in listing any of the recent behaviorally-oriented books is that a number of them may be overlooked. The reader should be alert to the fact that such studies represent the growing edges of research in geography, and publications of great value to the social studies teacher will undoubtedly be forthcoming in the near future.

Ecological Studies

One of the new directions in geographic research and publication in recent years, closely related to the behaviorally-oriented studies discussed in the preceding section, follows in the tradition of those geographers who have been concerned mainly with man-environment relations. Interested in ecological processes and ecosystems, a number of geographers have recently demonstrated that knowledge about the ways in which men perceive their external work areas helps to explain patterns of human behavior which heretofore have been poorly understood. Many of these studies deal with hazards, such as flooding or drought; others with differing attitudes towards resources and resource management, with environment, and with environmental pollution and control. Among these studies are **Resources and Man**, prepared by the Committee on Resources and Man of the Division of Earth Sciences, National Academy of Sciences-National Research Council (Freeman, 1969); and a book of readings entitled **Man's Impact on Environment,** edited by Thomas Detwyler (McGraw-Hill, 1971). Again, many books are being produced in the area of human ecology, and the social studies teacher needs to be aware of later, and perhaps even better, books in this area that will be published during the next several years.

Methodological Studies

For those teachers who are interested in the methods of inquiry used by modern geographers, there are a number of books which should be consulted from time to time. Popular among these are **Geography: Its Scope and Spirit,** by Jan O. M. Broek, Social Science Seminar Series, (Merrill, 1965, pb); **Frontiers in Geographical Teaching,** edited by Richard J. Chorley and Peter Haggett (Methuen, 1965, revised 1971); **Models in Geography,** a scholarly treatise by R. J. Chorley and P. Haggett (Methuen, 1967); **Spatial Analysis,** edited by Brian J. L. Berry and Duane F. Marble (Prentice-Hall, 1968); and a truly outstanding book, **Explanation in Geography** by David Harvey (St. Martin's 1969). Other books which discuss latest trends in geographic development include **Problems and Trends in American Geography,** edited by Saul B. Cohen (Basic, 1968); and **Focus on Geography,** edited by Phillip Bacon, (NCSS, 1970, pb). Each of these books provides the reader with modern perspectives in geography, and with geography as a field of inquiry. The latter also deals with teaching strategies.

Other books dealing with geographic education include **Geography in the Teaching of Social Studies: Concepts and Skills** by Hanna, Sabaroff, Davies, and Farrar (Houghton Mifflin, 1966); **The Teaching of Geography** by G. H. Gopsill (St. Martin's, 1966); and an especially fine report entitled **A Bibliography for Geographic Education,** compiled by John M. Ball, Research and Development Center in Educational Stimulation (Univ. of Georgia, No. 2, July, 1968). The last reference contains listings of bibliographies, and articles on Aims and Objectives, Values, Curriculum, Teaching Methods, Teacher Education, College and University Teaching, and Research in Geographic Education. More recently John M. Ball and John Steinbrink have edited a book entitled **The Social Sciences and Geographic Education: A Reader** (Wiley, 1971). Paul Hanna and other's **Geography in the Teaching of Social Studies** (Houghton Mifflin, 1966) stresses detailed and concrete examples for every elementary grade. Linnia James and LaMonte Crape's **Geography for Today's Children** (Appleton, 1968) also offers considerable practical help to the teacher with a slight background in geography. Most classroom teachers are aware, of course, of the *Journal of Geography,* published by the National Council for Geographic Education, Harm DeBlij, ed. A number of college-level textbooks are now beginning to appear which reflect modern trends in geographic education. Among these are **Spatial Organization: The Geographer's View of the World** by Abler, Adams, and Gould (Prentice-Hall, 1971) and Harm DeBlij's **Geography: Regions and Concepts** (Wiley, 1970).

5

United States History

RALPH ADAMS BROWN and MARIAN R. BROWN

It is difficult for the elementary school teacher, or the high school teacher of subjects other than history, to keep abreast of new books, ideas, and interpretations in the field of U.S. history. Yet both because the alert teacher must always try to keep informed of new ideas and trends in fields other than his own and because as citizens we should know of our own past, some reading in the field of U.S. history should be in the program of every teacher. The suggestions made below are for the non-specialist.

There are several magazines currently being published that are ideal for the teacher who would "dip" into the history of his own country, and yet who has neither the time nor the interest to read scholarly publications like the *Journal of American History.* Two such magazines are especially recommended and school and public libraries should have them both: *American Heritage* and *American History Illustrated.*

References and Large-Scope Sources

It is advisable for the reader of history to have an atlas at hand. Since so much of U.S. history is related to or dependent on events in other parts of the world, the suggested atlases include both those

---

Ralph Adams Brown is Professor of American History at the State University of New York, College at Cortland, New York; Marian R. Brown is a School Psychologist who has worked with her husband as both author and editor in the field of American history.

devoted solely to U.S. history and those with broader scope. There are special U.S. historical mappings in world atlases of Collier (Rand McNally). James Truslow Adams edited a very fine **Album of American History** (Scribner's, 1969) that is especially useful for those working with the major aspects of our nation's development. Clifford Lord and Elizabeth Lord produced a very useful guide in **Historical Atlas of the United States** (Johnson Reprint, 1969). Also valuable is **Atlas of American History** (Hammond, 1968, pb).

Illustrative works include the five-volume **Album of American History** (Scribner's, 1969), which remains the most complete work of its type. The much older **Pageant of America** series (in 15 volumes) contains much illustrative material; it is currently published by the United States Publishers Association. William C. Langdon's **Everyday Things in American Life,** 2 vols., (Scribner's, 1937, 1941) will prove very interesting to the general reader. R. Turner Wilcox's **Five Centuries of American Costume** (Scribner's, 1963) is a reference work of both interest and value.

Biographical guides include **The Concise Dictionary of American Biography** (Scribner's, 1964), which provides, in a single large volume, the essence of the 22-volume original which was the finest biographical compilation of this century. The late Clinton Rossiter's **The American Presidency** (Harcourt, 1966) is a provocative and highly readable work. Joseph Nathan Kane's **Facts About the Presidents; A Compilation of Biographical and Historical Data** (Wilson, 1967) can provide the general reader with illuminating data. Richard D. Lillard's **American Life in Autobiography** (Stanford Univ., 1961) is a useful reference work.

There are almost innumerable collections of sources and readings in U. S. history, most of them interesting and valuable. Three of them can be especially recommended: Richard C. Brown, ed., **The Human Side of American History** (Ginn, 1962, pb) is a small volume with an abundance of fascinating sidelights; two multi-volume collections that are rather inexpensive and very useful are six volumes in **A Documentary History of American Life** (McGraw-Hill, 1967, pb) and eight volumes of **Sources in American History** (Free Press, 1968, pb).

The Broad Scope of Our History

Seven volumes, all available in comparatively inexpensive paperback and that deal with large segments of the scope of our history, are recommended. Dixon Wecter's **The Hero in America** (Univ. of Michigan, 1963, pb) is an entertaining and yet authoritative treatment of prominent Americans from the days of John Smith to the New Deal. Alvin M. Josephy's **The Patriot Chiefs: A Chronicle of American Indian Leadership** (Viking, 1968, pb) offers unusual insight into seldom discussed Americans. The University of Chicago **History of American Civilization** series provides five paperbacks that deal with often neglected aspects of our national development. Quite concise and readable, they are: Richard M. Dorson, **American Folklore** (1959), John Tracy Ellis, **American Catholicism** (1969), Nathan Glazer, **American Judaism** (1957), William T. Hagan, **American Indians** (1961), and Henry Pelling, **American Labor** (1960), (all Univ. of Chicago, pb).

There are a number of useful books about the period from Christopher Columbus to Independence (1492-1783). For an understanding of the early English settlements in the seventeenth and eighteenth centuries, there are three books that are both accurate and colorful: Carl Becker, **The Beginnings of the American People;** Thomas J. Wertenbaker, **The Golden Age of American Culture;** and Louis B. Wright, **The Atlantic Frontier** (all from Cornell Univ., 1960, 1959, 1963, pb). Military events in the struggle for the New World are well covered in Howard H. Peckham, **The Colonial Wars, 1689-1762** (Univ. of Chicago, 1964, pb). Moving into the period of the Revolution and the struggle for independence, Edmund S. Morgan's **The Birth of the Republic, 1763-1789** (Univ. of Chicago, 1956, pb) provides a brief but often fascinating account of the movement for independence and the political events of the years between 1775 and 1789. The Revolution on the frontier, a topic often ignored, is set forth with brilliance and excitement by Dale Van Every in **A Company of Heroes, The American Frontier, 1775-1783** (New American Library, 1963, pb). Two provocative books that deal with the efforts to form a new government are Wesley F. Craven's **The Legend of the Founding Fathers** (Cornell Univ., 1965, pb) and Adrienne Koch's **Power, Morals, and the Founding Fathers** (Cornell Univ., 1961, pb).

From a new nation to a nation saved (1783-1865) is the focus of other perceptive books. Gilbert Chinard's **Honest John Adams** (Little, Brown, 1933, pb) has been called the best one-volume biography of our second President, and Henry Adams' **The United States in 1800** (Cornell Univ., 1955, pb) is a brilliant description of our country at the turn of the century. The frontier has always had a strong fascination for Americans, and the stories of the westward progress of our people are often illuminating. Five books dealing with this area are recommended: Bernard De Voto's **Across the Wide Missouri** and his **Year of Decision** (both Houghton Mifflin, 1947, 1950, pb) are graphic and accurate. David Lavender's **Westward Vision: The Oregon Trail** (McGraw-Hill, 1963) is part of a fascinating series called the **American Trails Series.** Dale Van Every's **The Final Challenge: The American Frontier, 1804-1845** (Morrow, 1964) has never been surpassed and seldom equalled for its intensity and drama. Jay Monaghan's **The Book of the American West** (Simon & Schuster, 1963) is a huge volume, profusely and beautifully illustrated, that considers almost every imaginable aspect of the westward movement.

Charles M. Wiltse's **The New Nation, 1800-1845** (Hill and Wang, 1961, pb) is part of a series that surveys our history for the lay reader; it is concise and readable. E. Douglas Branch's **The Sentimental Years** (Hill and Wang, 1965, pb) offers some rather unusual insights into the early nineteenth century. Henrietta Buckmaster's **Let My People Go** (Beacon, 1959, pb) is a "must" for those who would understand the role of the Negro in our history. Two of the many excellent biographies of important leaders during the second quarter of the nineteenth century are Gerald M. Capers' **Stephen A. Douglas, Defender of the Union** (Little, Brown, 1959) and Margaret Coit's **John C. Calhoun, American Portrait** (Houghton Mifflin, 1950, pb).

Among the hundreds of interesting books dealing with the years of the Civil War are two by Bell Irwin Wiley—both have been out of print but were recently republished: **The Life of Billy Yank** and **The Life of Johnny Reb** (Doubleday, 1971).

From reunion to world power (1865-1920) is an era of interest to many authors. John Hope Franklin's **Reconstruction: After the Civil War** (Univ. of Chicago, 1961, pb) is a readable and reliable account of the years of turmoil and strife that followed the War for the Union; Franklin is one of the nation's leading historians. Samuel P. Hays' **The Response to Industrialism** (Univ. of Chicago, 1957, pb) provides an excellent record of our industrial growth and of the economic and social problems that stemmed from industrialism. Oscar Handlin's **The American People in the 20th Century** (Beacon, 1963, pb) and John R. Blum's **Woodrow Wilson and the Politics of Morality** (Little, Brown, 1956, pb) offer the lay reader opportunities to increase his understanding of the events and issues of the first two decades of this century.

From world leadership to the present (1920-1970) is a period that is analyzed in a variety of ways. Barbara Habenstreit's **Eternal Vigilance, The American Civil Liberties Union in Action** (Messner, 1971) gives the record of action and achievement of an organization that has played a leading role in the fight for individual freedom. Michael Harrington's **The Other America: Poverty in the United States** (Penguin, 1963, pb) should be read by all thoughtful Americans. Dexter Perkins' **The New Age of Franklin Roosevelt, 1932-1945** (Univ. of Chicago, 1957, pb) is an extremely readable account of the New Deal years by an articulate and somewhat biased historian. Walter Johnson's **1600 Pennsylvania Avenue** (Little, Brown, 1960, pb) emphasizes and interprets the role of presidential leadership in this century. David Weingast's **We Elect a President** (Messner, 1968) offers the non-specialist a simple, painless, and accurate introduction to the election process. Samuel Eliot Morison's **Two-Ocean War** (Little, Brown, 1963, pb) is a brilliant account of the naval aspect of World War II. Morison is one of the stylistic leaders among American historians, and a sailor with combat experience in World War II.

Guides for Teaching U.S. History

Teachers more deeply interested in United States history will turn to several sources that are available in most libraries. Among these are: Ralph Adams Brown and Marian Brown, eds., **American History Book List for High Schools** (NCSS, 1969, pb); William H. Cartwright and Richard L. Watson, eds., **Interpreting and Teaching American History** (NCSS, 1961, pb); and Leonard B. Irwin, ed., **Guide to Historical Reading: Nonfiction** (McKinley, 1970). This last book covers the entire range of history, but has over 100 pages devoted to U. S. history.

Teaching of History by Henry Johnson (Macmillan, 1940) is still available. Henry S. Commager's **The Nature and the Study of History** (Merrill, 1965) is a concise and readable description of the nature of history, its methods and fundamental ideas.

The New Social Studies for the Slow Learner (American Heritage, 1969), by the staff of the Social Studies Curriculum Center at Carnegie-Mellon University, provides a rationale for a new American history course designed for inquiry teaching of slow learners in junior high school. C. L. Lord, ed., **Teaching History with Community Resources** (Columbia Univ., 1964, pb) is useful. The November 1971 issue of *Social Education* is devoted to the teaching of United States history. The articles deal with a variety of ways to improve the teaching of United State history.

David F. Kellum's **American History Through Conflicting Interpretations** (Teachers College, Columbia, 1969) provides a rationale for a problems-centered approach to American history. The problems are conflicting interpretations of major developments in the American past (e.g., "Reconstruction: Exploitation of the South or Genuine Reform?"), and nine such problems are developed, along with teachers' methodological suggestions. Lawrence A. Fink's **Honors Teaching in American History** (Teachers College, Columbia, 1969) is an account of a high school honors course taught by the author. The focus of the course was on historical method and the critical analysis and evaluation of primary sources and interpretative materials by historians.

Major historical works dealing with social injustice and cultural minorities are cited elsewhere in this book. Consult the Table of Contents for guidelines to materials in these areas.

6

World History

DOUGLAS D. ALDER

A teacher of world history would be well served to have some general histories at his elbow. Two volumes by William H. McNeill seem preëminent, **The Rise of the West: A History of the Human Community** (Univ. of Chicago Press, 1963, pb) and **A World History** (Oxford Univ., 1967), which is a briefer approach of the same viewpoint. A classic college text of rigorous standards is R. R. Palmer's **A History of the Modern World** (Knopf, 1970). Its bias is both modern and western. Two contributing authors are also helpful, Morris Gall and Arthur Soderlind, eds., **World Civilization Booklist** and Shirley H. Engle, ed., **New Perspectives in World History** (NCSS, 1968, 1964, pb).

Some other reference tools for the teaching profession are the pamphlets produced by the Service Center for Teachers of History (American Historical Assn.). They are brief and focus on major topics throughout the whole range of world history. Similarly a series of pamphlets produced by the Historical Association in England provide capsules of palatable bibliographic insight for teachers. A good historical atlas is a valued companion. W. R. Shepherd's **Historical Atlas** (Barnes & Noble, 1964) is a standard. Historical journals are numerous, but for this subject *American Historical Review* (Washington, D.C.) appears the ultimate in scholarship and weight while *History Today* (London) seems refreshing and colorful.

Douglas D. Alder is Associate Director for Instructional Improvement, and Associate Professor of History, Utah State University, Logan, Utah.

Non-Western World Regions

Beyond the general tools teachers will have to virtually tour the historiographic world to become informed on the vast subject of world history. Starting with almost a new field, Africa is now the subject of wide attention. In the 1960's Roland Oliver and J. D. Fage's book, **Short History of Africa** (Penguin, 1966) was the basic introduction. Robert July's **History of the African People** (Scribner's, 1970) includes more current research. Basil Davidson's **Lost Cities of Africa** (Atlantic Monthly, 1959, pb) is a popular account of the early sub-Saharan civilizations while Desmond Clark's **Pre-History of Africa** (Grossman, 1970) carries the subject to an earlier, pre-literate age. For South Africa's particular problem, Apartheid, Leonard Thompson's **Politics in the Republic of South Africa** (Little, Brown, 1966, pb) gives an historian's view of the contemporary problem.

For North Africa and the Middle East Bernard Lewis' **Arabs in History** (Torch, 1950, pb) is an excellent short survey. Philip K. Hitti's scholarly work is available as the **History of the Arabs** or in a popular version **Arabs: A Short History** (St. Martin, 1963, 1969, pb). H. A. R. Gibb's **Mohammedanism: An Historical Survey** (Oxford Univ., 1962, pb) is an approach to the most influential factor in the Middle East. A dated objective background to the tensions of the present Middle East is George Lenczowski, **The Middle East in World Affairs** (Cornell Univ., 1962, pb). George Ostrogorsky, **History of the Byzantine State** (Rutgers Univ., 1969) and L. S. Stavrianos, **The Balkans Since 1453** (Harper & Row, 1958) introduce the transition area between Europe and the Middle East.

India's history is so extensive that the general teacher will likely need a general study. Percival Spear, **India, A Modern History** (Univ. of Michigan, 1961) serves that purpose. Another way to approach that rich culture is through the two volumes edited by William Theodore de Bary, **Sources of Indian Tradition** (Columbia Univ., 1969).

Edwin O. Reischauer and John K. Fairbank introduce the great traditional oriental culture in **East Asia: The Great Tradition.** A companion volume, Reischauer and Albert M. Craig, **East Asia: The Modern Transformation** (Houghton Mifflin, 1958, 1965), completes the set to make up the most comprehensive, balanced history of East Asia (including China, Japan, Korea, and Southeast Asia) in the English language. Immanuel C. Y. Hsü, **The Rise of Modern China** (Oxford Univ., 1970), is a detailed study beginning with the Manchu dynasty. Edmund O. Clubb (once controversial U.S. State Department official) presents **Twentieth Century China** (Columbia Univ., 1964, pb). Kenneth Scott Latourette represents the "old China hands" in his standard work **The Chinese: Their History and Culture** (Macmillan, 1964). Three recommended works on modern Japan are: John W. Hall and Richard K. Beardsley, **Twelve**

Doors to Japan (McGraw-Hill, 1965); W. G. Beasley, **Modern History of Japan** (Praeger, 1963, pb); and Edwin O. Reischauer, **United States and Japan** (Viking, 1962, pb). Two syllabi that are helpful to teachers are: J. Mason Gentzler, **Syllabus of Chinese Civilization;** and Paul Varley, **Syllabus of Japanese Civilization** (Columbia Univ., 1968, pbs).

Moving quickly southeast one can pause to read John B. Condliffe's **Development of Australia** (Free Press, 1964) or Condliffe and Willis T. G. Airey, **Short History of New Zealand** (Tri-Ocean, 1966). By reversing Thor Heyerdahl one arrives in Latin America. Here Hubert Herring's **History of Latin America** (Knopf, 1968) is a good introduction. Frank Tannenbaum, **Ten Keys to Latin America** (Knopf, 1962) is another general work from a North American, whereas Jacques Lambert, **Latin America: Social Structure and Political Institutions** (Univ. of California, 1968) gives an important view from a French viewpoint.

Western World Regions

To begin an examination of Western Civilization one should start with the great ancient civilizations. John A. Wilson, **The Burden of Egypt** (Univ. of Chicago, 1951) is a warm but authoritative treatment. Readers should also look at the classic **History of Egypt from the Earliest Times to the Persian Conquest** (Bantam, 1909, 1964, pb) by James H. Breasted. Tigris-Euphrates Valley has been the fertile host to succeeding civilizations. Samuel N. Kramer, **History Begins at Sumer** (Anchor, 1959) is a social introduction to that ancient civilizaton. George Contenau, **Everyday Life in Babylonia and Assyria** (Norton, 1966) is also an excellent general introduction to these societies.

As the major formative influence of the West the Greco-Roman culture deserves special attention. J. B. Bury's old work is still respected: **History of Greece** (Modern Library, 1908, 1959). A more recent and forceful short work is Mikhail Rostovtzeff, **Greece** (Oxford Univ., 1963, pb). Another respected book is Fustel de Coulanges, **The Ancient City** (Anchor Doubleday, 1873, pb). A light and sympathetic introduction is H. D. Kitto's **Greeks** (Penguin, 1951, pb). For the Hellenistic period much of the debate centers around W. W. Tarn, **Alexander the Great** (Beacon, 1956, pb). Teachers should involve their students with the Great Greek classics, **The Iliad** and **The Odyssey.** Most students can be fascinated by Greek drama such as **Oedipus Rex** or **Antigone.** Serious students can enjoy Thucydides, **Peloponnesian Wars** and Herodotus, **Persian Wars.** All of these original works are available in many editions and in anthologies in Modern Library and other publications.

Theodore Mommsen, **History of Rome** is available in a Meridian paper edition (1958) as an abridgement of the great nineteenth-century German scholar's multivolume classic. The Meridian account concentrates on the Late Republic. Ronald Syme's **Roman Revolution** (Oxford

Univ., 1960, pb) is another great work on that crucial period. More recent scholarship specifically for Rome has produced M. Cary's **History of Rome** (St. Martin's, 1954) and M. Rostovtzeff, **Rome** (Oxford Univ., 1960). For some original Roman writing students would find Caesar or Livy appropriate.

The "most Christian Epoch" — the Middle Ages — holds fascination if it can be unlocked for students. Norman F. Cantor, **Medieval History** (Macmillan, 1969) gives an impressive overview. Human interest and social history that departs from the idealizing about the Medieval period can be found in G. G. Coulton's works: **Medieval Panorama** (Cambridge, 1969, pb). For a solid look at the intellectual life, H. O. Taylor's two volumes, **The Medieval Mind** (Harvard Univ., 1959), though old, are still widely used. Carl Stephenson's small booklet **Medieval Feudalism** (Cornell Univ., 1942, pb) describes the political system. Henri Pirenne's thesis about Medieval trade and his writings are the center of the controversy about Medieval economics. **Economic and Social History of Medieval Europe** (Harvard Univ., 1937, pb) and **Medieval Cities: Their Origins and the Revival of Trade** (Princeton Univ., 1925, pb) outline his views which are challenged by several more recent authors. Religion was the lifeblood of the Medieval society. Two ways to approach that subject are Philip Hughes, **A Popular History of the Catholic Church** (Image, 1947, Macmillan, 1970, pb) for a Catholic view, and Henry Adams, **Mont-Saint-Michel and Chartres** (Doubleday, 1905, 1959, pb) for a cultural idealistic view by one of America's most gifted historians.

One good way to build a transition from Medieval to Modern is to examine the history of science. Herbert Butterfield, **The Origins of Modern Science 1300-1800** (Free Press, 1965) does just that, whereas A. Rupert Hall and Marie Boas Hall, **A Brief History of Science** (Signet, 1964, pb) gives a view of the subject which includes a longer perspective, starting with the Greeks, and continuing through the mid-twentieth century. A more traditional way to make the transition is to debate the issue concerning whether there was, in fact, a Renaissance. C. H. Haskins, **Renaissance of the 12th Century** (Meridian, 1927, 1965, pb) argues the gradualist point whereas the classic by Jacob Burckhardt, **The Civilization of the Renaissance in Italy** (Mentor, 1860, pb), started a major debate on the side of a unique rebirth of classical culture. Wallace K. Ferguson, **The Renaissance in Historical Thought: Five centuries of Interpretation** (Houghton Mifflin, 1948) balances both views.

A judicious way to balance the Reformation is to read Roland Bainton's **Reformation of the Sixteenth Century** (Beacon, 1956, pb) or **Here I Stand: a Life of Martin Luther** (Mentor, 1950, pb) with Father Philip Hughes, ed., **A Popular History of the Reformation** (Doubleday, 1969, pb). Erik Erikson's **Young Man Luther** (Norton, 1958, pb) provides as much fun for its psychoanalytical approach as for its information.

The thrust of Western Civilization outward to dominate the rest of the planet is one of the most sobering of modern phenomena. It continues today through the industrialization developed in the west. Samuel Eliot Morison, **Admiral of the Ocean Sea: a Life of Christopher Columbus** (Atlantic Monthly, 1942) is a seafarer's classic capturing the beginning of that expansion. J. H. Parry, **Age of Reconnaissance** (Praeger, 1970, pb) is more recent and more inclusive. Of all the studies that could represent the two centuries of building great nations and dynasties, the following three will have to suffice: J. E. Neale, **Queen Elizabeth First** (Anchor Doubleday, 1957, pb), Garrett Mattingly, **The Armada** (Houghton Mifflin, 1959), and Gerhart Ritter, **Frederick the Great** (Univ. of California, 1968).

The end of the great dynasties can be seen as the French Revolution ushers in popular sovereignty and mass society. Alexis de Tocqueville, **The Old Regime and the French Revolution** (Anchor Doubleday, 1955, pb) conducts the aristocracy out with nostalgia. Georges Lefebvre, **French Revolution** (Columbia Univ., 1962) 2 vols., gives the best from the French view. Robert R. Palmer's **Age of the Democratic Revolution** (Princeton Univ., 1959) gives an international synthesis to the revolutionary epoch. J. M. Thompson, **Napoleon Bonaparte: His Rise and Fall** (Oxford Univ., 1952, pb) concludes the revolution.

The Industrial Revolution has been briefly summarized by T. S. Ashton, **The Industrial Revolution 1790-1830** (Oxford Univ., 1948, pb). The resulting socialism is nicely introduced in Martin Buber, **Paths in Utopia** (Beacon, 1958, pb). Isaiah Berlin's **Karl Marx, His Life and Environment** (Oxford Univ., 1963, pb) and Alfred G. Meyer's **Communism** (Random House, 1967, pb) give balanced accounts. World War I is treated in René Albrecht-Carrie's brief work: **Meaning of the First World War** (Spectrum, 1965, pb).

Russia and Modern Communism are generally treated in secondary schools. Teachers would do well to use the following works for their information: Nicholas V. Riasanovsky, **A History of Russia** (Oxford Univ., 1969), Donald W. Treadgold, **Twentieth Century Russia** (Rand McNally, 1964), and Adam B. Ulam, **The Bolsheviks** (Macmillan, 1968, pb).

Gordon Wright, **France in Modern Times, 1760 to the Present** (Rand McNally, 1960) is beautifully written and includes excellent bibliographic essays. Koppel Pinson, **Modern Germany** (Macmillan, 1966) is the best one-volume general work on Germany. England will not settle for a one-volume treatment. The scholarly way to study Great Britain is via **Oxford History of England** (Clarendon), a 14-volume series edited by Sir George Clark. Each volume is written by a major scholar. A lighter but worthwhile approach is the **Pelican History of England** (Pelican), consisting of eight paperback volumes by different authors. Even more concise is G. M. Trevelyan's three-volume paperback **History of England** (Doubleday, 1926-1952, pb). Winston Churchill, **History of the English-Speaking People** (Dodd, 1956), is first-class historical journalism.

For Europe specifically in the twentieth century one can focus on the crisis brought by Totalitarianism. Alan Bullock, **Hitler, A Study in Tyranny** (Harper, 1962) is solid and inclusive. Carl J. Friedrich and Zbigniew K. Brzezinski, **Totalitarian Dictatorship and Autocracy** (Harvard Univ., 1965) deals with the concept from both German and Russian directions.

A general work that is helpful for all of European history is Herbert Heaton, **An Economic History of Europe** (Harper & Row, 1948). A most thorough approach would be to systematically study **The Rise of Modern Europe** (Harper & Row, pb) series edited by William L. Langer. Each volume is written by a major scholar and includes a fine bibliographical essay. **The New Cambridge Modern History** (Cambridge Univ.) planned by Sir George Clark is still another great cooperative set. Another exciting approach would be to read the great memoirs. The major ones would include those by Napoleon, Bismarck, and De Gaulle.

7

Psychology

JUDITH V. TORNEY

Psychology as a social science is relatively new to many high schools. The biological bases of behavior have often been included in biology courses, though the link between neurological processes and psychological ones is often lacking. Some aspects of psychology as a social science have been treated within units on marriage and the family or courses called social problems. Psychologists, however, feel rather strongly that even at relatively basic levels of study it is important to introduce students to major elements of psychology as a discipline — learning processes, psychological development and motivation — rather than focusing only upon psychological adjustment or social behavior. To view only man's social interactions without considering psychological processes which influence them presents an incomplete picture of man and of psychologists' attempts to understand him.

A major source of information for all high school teachers of psychology, **Program on the Teaching of Psychology in the Secondary School** (American Psychological Assn., 1970, pb), includes an extensive annotated bibliography of introductory books suitable for assignment to high school students, of books of readings, and of audiovisual aids. This review will update some of the APA suggestions, go into some areas in greater depth, and offer some materials which would be useful to teachers of psychology to strengthen their background but would be too advanced for high school students.

Judith V. Torney is Associate Professor, College of Education and Department of Psychology, University of Illinois at Chicago Circle, Chicago, Illinois.

Introduction and General References

From among the many introductory texts, three books are included because of the eminence of the psychologists who wrote them, the breadth and depth of their coverage, and their focus upon current psychological research: F. H. Sanford and L. S. Wrightsman, **Psychology: A Scientific Study of Man** (Brooks/Cole, 1970, pb); D. Krech, Crutchfield and Livson, **Elements of Psychology** (Knopf, 1969, pb); and Ernest R. Hilgard and Atkinson, **Introduction to Psychology** (Harcourt, 1967).

Collections of articles from professional periodicals portray psychology as a living discipline. R. A. King, ed., **Readings for an Introduction to Psychology** (McGraw-Hill, 1966) has collected papers important in understanding the structure and development of psychology as a discipline. Richard Atkinson, ed., **Contemporary Psychology** (Freeman, 1971) presents readings from the *Scientific American,* written without jargon but with careful attention to the scientific nature of psychology. In a slightly different vein are a series of readings put together around the concerns of young people: Nicholas Pronko, ed., **Panorama of Psychology** (Brooks/Cole, 1969, pb); R. V. Guthrie, ed., **Psychology in the World Today** (Addison-Wesley, 1968, pb).

Short abstracts inventory generalizations which can reliably be made from psychological research – usually replicated by different investigators in different settings. The major publication reviewing current thinking is **Annual Review of Psychology** (Annual Reviews). It presents short review articles summarizing a year's research in each major area of psychology; a recent volume included Personality, Developmental Psychology, and Behavior Therapy (to mention only three chapters).

This review will concentrate on social, learning, cognitive personality, and developmental psychology because of insufficient space to deal with every area of psychology. Although students may not obtain a fully balanced view of the discipline, they should realize that in addition to the psychology they see applied in fads of the day (like encounter groups), psychology is a behavioral science which seeks understanding of human processes of thinking, learning, growing, and relating to others.

Learning and Cognition

One problem faced by students in the study of learning is that they see it only in the context of the school and find it difficult to view competing theories or explanations. E. R. Hilgard and Bowers, **Theories of Learning** (Appleton, 1966) is a classic reference which compares and evaluates every currently prominent theory about the learning process in animals and humans. It is a next-to-final authority on learning theories (if one cannot consult primary sources). Walter Kintsch, **Learning, Memory and Conceptual Processes** (Wiley, 1970) is a balanced presentation of various types of human learning performance: standard experiments, decision and organizational processes in memory, and concept identification. It is a lengthy volume but one which deals with the historical antecedents as well as the current view of learning in the human animal. C. B. Ferster and Parrott, **Behavior Principles** (Appleton, 1967, pb) has served as a basis for much current work in behavior modification. Students need to understand that the application of psychology in such programs is usually preceded for several years by discussion of the basic theory by psychologists. Uric Neisser, **Cognition** (Appleton, 1967) contains a detailed, up-to-date, and well organized discussion of thinking. Jerome Bruner, Goodnow and Austin, **A Study of Thinking** (Wiley, 1956, pb) represents an early trendsetting study. It emphasizes strategies people use when they engage in complex mental activity. A series in the general area of learning and cognition is F. A. Logan and Wagner, **Reward and Punishment,** Lyle Bourne, **Human Conceptual Behavior,** James Deese, **Psycholinguistics** (all Allyn & Bacon, 1965, 1966, 1970, pbs).

Psychology of Personality

Teachers can find ready reference to mental health through education psychology texts. This review deals with the study of personality and theories as to its structure rather than with questions of normality and adjustment. The basic text, I. L. Janis, Mahl, Kagan, and Holt, **Personality: Dynamics, Development, and Assessment** (Harcourt, 1969) is also divided into four paperbacks by major topic — Stress and Frustration, Psychological Conflict and Defense, Personality Development, and Assessing Personality. Four alternative viewpoints in the study of personality (biological, experimental, social and psychometric trait) are presented in J. S. Wiggins, Renner, Clore and Rose, **The Psychology of Personality** (Addison-Wesley, 1971). Each viewpoint is then applied to the study of dependency, aggression, sexuality and competence. C. S. Hall and Lindzey, **Theories of Personality** (Wiley, 1970) represents to the field of personality what Hilgard and Bowers represents for theories of learning. Hall and Lindzey, in other words, is the standard reference (next to primary sources), for the comparison of theories. Each theory is introduced with its history followed by the structure, dynamics and development of personality, and a critique. These authors present a wide variety of theoretical positions with realism and without favoritism. Harry Kaufmann, **Aggression and Altruism: A Psychological Analysis** and Kenneth Gergen, **The Concept of Self** (both Holt, 1971, pbs) could supplement these particular topics. Robert Goldenson, **The Encyclopedia of Human Behavior: Psychology, Psychiatry and Mental Health** (Doubleday, 1970) is an unusual example of an encyclopedia written by a single individual. About two-thirds of the contents relate to topics in the study of personality and mental health. The book is authoritative yet suitable for a reader with a relatively minimal background in psychology.

Among a sudden rush of books on encounter groups, Arthur Burton, ed., **Encounter** (Jossey-Bass, 1969) has been reasonably well received as a useful introduction to the experience. Even reading several such volumes, however, will not prepare the teacher to deal adequately with all the ramifications of using the technique. A book which may help the teacher to understand herself is A. H. Maslow, **Motivation and Personality** (Harper and Row, 1954). Julian Rotter, **Clinical Psychology** (Prentice-Hall, 1971, pb), meets an important need by defining the role and task of the clinical psychologist as distinct, for example, from a psychiatrist. He covers assessment of intelligence and of personality as well as psychotherapy, continuing with a brief review of theoretical approaches to personality.

Social Psychology

Several subareas of psychology can serve as focal points for viewing other subareas of the discipline. Visualize an eight-sided hinged screen (with mirror sides on each end portion) which can be folded in several ways to allow either of two different portions to appear inside as a reflector of the other seven sides. Social and developmental psychology can be seen as these reflecting links through which learning, perception, and personality can be viewed. For example, social psychology uses cognitive theory in understanding social attitudes and their changes; it reflects a new perspective for cognitive theory in the process. Some of the best general books in social psychology are outstanding precisely because they reflect other subdisciplines.

From the title of the book by Roger Brown, **Social Psychology** (Free Press, 1965), one might expect a standard text introduction. It is, in fact, a volume in which social psychology is viewed in the fashion outlined above, with insight as well as experiment. It sets a variety of areas into the context of social psychology (e.g., child language development and socialization). Barry Collins, **Social Psychology** (Addison-Wesley, 1970) covers a variety of topics in social psychology—describing key experiments and highlighting some resolutions to problems. James Schellenberg, **An Introduction to Social Psychology** (Random House, 1970) has both relatively standard topics (aggression, attitude change, group behavior) and others less often included (the relation of the young child to the environment, ethical problems in research). He introduces each topic with a case study. There is also a series of outstanding paperbacks in social psychology, Charles Keisler, **Conformity;** Ellen Berscheid and Elaine C. Walster, **Interpersonal Attraction;** James Davis, **Group Performance;** Kenneth Gergen, **The Psychology of Behavior Exchange;** Albert Hastorf, **Person Perception;** Karl Weick, **The Social Psychology of Organizing;** P. G. Zimbardo and E. B. Ebbesen, **Influencing Attitudes and Changing Behavior** (all Addison-Wesley, all 1969). Each is written by a psychologist who has done extensive work in the area. Daryl Bem, **Beliefs, Attitudes, and Human Affairs** (Brooks/Cole, 1970, pb), also presents a straightforward conceptualization of the relationship between elements of attitudes and beliefs. Two recent collections of readings deal with current social problems. Michael Wertheimer, ed., **Confrontation: Psychology and the Problems of Today** (Scott, Foresman, 1970) uses graphics as well as text. Richard I. Evans and Richard M. Rozelle, **Social Psychology in Life** (Allyn & Bacon, 1970) presents both participant and experimental studies of current interest. Abe Arkoff, **Explorations in Human Behavior** (McGraw-Hill, 1971) gives tasks and exercises (e.g., attitude measurement scales) which precede rather than follow expository material, helping to concretize ideas about psychological research.

The five volumes of Gardner Lindzey and Aronson, eds., **The Handbook of Social Psychology,** are an indispensable reference. The individual volumes consider: I. **Historical Introduction, Systematic Positions,** II. **Research Methods,** III. **The Individual in a Social Context,** IV. **Group Psychology and Phenomena of Interaction,** V. **Applied Social Psychology** (all Addison-Wesley, 1968, 1968, 1969, 1969, 1969). This is a revision of 1935 and 1954 handbooks demonstrating, among other things, the growth of the discipline and the increased importance of experimental work in social psychology. Teachers who wish to explore any social psychological topic in depth can profitably begin here.

E. Webb, Campbell, Schwartz and Sechrest, **Unobtrusive Measures: Non-Reactive Research in the Social Sciences** (Rand McNally, 1966, pb) represents a reaction against this increasing stress in social psychology upon experimental laboratory studies. This volume proposes that measures of social behavior which can be collected in natural social situations, often without the knowledge of the participants, are a critical balance for the field. Bibb Latane and John M. Darley, **The Unresponsive Bystander: Why Doesn't He Help?** (Appleton, 1970) is part of a current trend toward studies which take a phenomenon from the real world and translate it, with appropriate controls, into the laboratory for study. This book will interest many who are not academic psychologists because of human concern for the problem it poses. Marvin Karlins and Abelson, **Persuasion: How Opinions and Attitudes Are Changed** (Springer, 1970, pb) delineates the practical principles of persuasion. Each section begins with questions (e.g., "How well do you have to know a person before he can influence your behavior?") and provides some answers and several brief descriptions of supporting experiments.

Developmental Psychology

Developmental psychology, like social, serves as a reflecting and refining point for studies of learning processes, social interactions, and cognitive abilities. Students from the beginning of their study should be aware that developmental psychology is not concerned only with describing the average three-year-old but rather with understanding the important factors or processes by which change occurs over time. Paul Mussen, Conger and Kagen, **Child Development and Personality** (Harper & Row, 1969) carries the child through adolescence with substantial research included. L. Joseph Stone and Church, **Childhood and Adolescence: A Psychology of the Growing Person** (Random House, 1968) covers the same age period with less research emphasis. The book by Hayne Reese and Lipsitt, **Experimental Child Psychology** (Academic Press, 1970) illustrates the sense in which developmental psychology reflects and utilizes other branches of the discipline. The book considers topics such as sensory processes, conditioning, language acquisition from the experimental psychological point of view. Jerome Kagan, **Understanding Children** (Harcourt, 1971, pb) considers motivation, cognitive and intellectual development with sensitivity, carefully drawing implications for teaching and learning. Muriel Beadle, **A Child's Mind** (Doubleday, 1971) is written for a non-professional audience but summarizes major implications of recent research. Paul Mussen, ed., **Carmichael's Manual of Child Psychology** (Wiley, 1970) includes relatively short research-based discussions formulated by respected authorities under general headings such as Infancy and Early Experience, Cognitive Development, and Socialization. There is a 30-page summary of Piaget by Piaget, and a section on cross-cultural study in child psychology, to name only two of 29 selections. This is an appropriate source for authoritative statements.

John Flavell, **The Developmental Psychology of Jean Piaget** (Van Nostrand, 1963) is a relatively complete summary—a help for one who has reasonably well-formulated questions to resolve about Piaget's theory. Ginsburg and Opper, **Piaget's Theory of Intellectual Development: An Introduction** (Prentice-Hall, 1969, pb) is a more compact and less technical summary. Erik Erickson in **Childhood and Society** (Norton, 1951) presents a theory which has served durably for relating the behavior of children to social demands and for portraying the particular character of adolescence. Gerald Lesser, ed., has included in **Psychology and Educational Practice** (Scott Foresman, 1971) chapters by prominent psychologists to help those involved in the teaching process to see the role of psychological insights in shaping learning. Individualized instruction, analysis of children's errors, and moral development are three of the topics covered.

Finally, guides which students may find helpful are **A Career in Psychology** (American Psychological Assn., 1970) and Theodore Sarbin, **The Students Psychologist's Handbook: A Guide to Sources** (Schenkman, 1969, pb).

8

Political Science

JOHN J. PATRICK

An explosive development of knowledge and techniques of inquiry has marked the recent work of social scientists interested in political phenomena. During the past thirty years, students of politics have increasingly extended the scope of their inquiries to include the political behavior of individuals and small groups as well as large structures such as nations, parties, and legal systems. Basic concepts of sociologists, anthropologists, and social psychologists, such as culture, society, socialization, role, status, and personality, have been used to study relationships between political behaviors, political processes, and socio-cultural contexts. Statistical analyses of individual and aggregate data, derived from random sample surveys and governmental records, have yielded more complex and profound understandings of political behavior and the workings of political institutions.

The Study of Politics

Changes in the questions, techniques of inquiry, and research findings of political scientists are discussed in Francis J. Sorauf, **Political Science: An Informal Overview** (Merrill, 1965, pb). The behavioral approach to the study of politics, which has been fundamental to recent developments in political science, is discussed succinctly in Heinz Eulau, **The Behavioral Persuasion in Politics** (Random House, 1963, pb). Controversies surrounding the use of the behavioral approach in political

---

John J. Patrick is Co-director of the High School Political Science Curriculum Project, Indiana University, Bloomington, Indiana.

science are presented in Heinz Eulau, ed., **Behavioralism in Political Science** (Atherton, 1969). Robert Dahl, **Modern Political Analysis** (Prentice-Hall, 1963, pb) is a brief introduction to questions and conceptual frameworks of the modern political scientist. A collection of articles from political and related social sciences broadens the field of **The Learning of Political Behavior,** Norman Alder and Charles Harrington, eds. (Scott, Foresman, 1970). A more recent book is **American Political Behavior** by Howard D. Mehlinger and John J. Patrick (Ginn, 1972).

The Socio-Cultural Bases of Politics

The socio-cultural bases of politics is the focus of S. M. Lipset, **Political Man** (Doubleday, 1960, pb). Lipset discusses the relationships of social structures and culture to the development of democratic political institutions. Don R. Bowen, **Political Behavior of the American Public** (Merrill, 1968, pb) presents research findings about the relationships of culture, socialization, social class, role, and personality to political behavior. Variation in the political activity of different types of individuals and groups is the subject of Lester W. Milbrath, **Political Participation** (Rand McNally, 1965, pb).

Milbrath reviews recent research that indicates the relationships of social and personal factors to involvement in politics. The relationship of public opinion to political behavior is discussed in Robert E. Lane and David O. Sears, **Public Opinion** (Prentice-Hall, 1964, pb). Research about the process of acquiring political attitudes is reviewed in Richard E. Dawson and Kenneth Prewitt, **Political Socialization** (Little, Brown, 1969, pb).

Community Power Structures

Studies of community power structures are a special category of inquiries about the relationships of socio-cultural factors to public policy-making. The community power analysts have considered questions about who holds political power, how this power was acquired, and how this power is used. Arnold M. Rose, **The Power Structure** (Oxford Univ., 1967) reviews numerous studies of public opinion, the political behavior of masses and leaders, and public policy-making to refute the arguments of scholars, such as C. Wright Mills, who have contended that a small elite controls political life in the United States. The author concludes that various groups wield power in many different ways. Depending upon particular circumstances, which vary from situation to situation, different groups may or may not attain their objectives. Case studies of different groups attempting to exert political pressure are presented as illustrations of the author's main arguments. Robert A.

Dahl, **Who Governs?** (Yale Univ., 1961, pb) is another argument, based on an empirical study of political participation and public policymaking in New Haven, Connecticut, that the bases of political power shift from issue to issue as various groups contend and compromise with each other. The author convincingly articulates a pluralist theory of community politics in contrast to the proponents of elitist or monolithic power structure theories. A comprehensive view of the findings and methodologies of community power research is presented in Willis Hawley and Frederick Wirt, eds., **The Search for Community Power** (Prentice-Hall, 1968, pb). This is a series of readings which discuss the various major approaches to the study of urban politics.

Voter Behavior and Public Elections

Much important research about voter behavior and public elections has been conducted during the past thirty years. These research findings are reviewed in William H. Flanigan, **Political Behavior of the American Electorate** (Allyn and Bacon, 1968, pb). Flanigan discusses findings pertinent to questions about the variation in participation in election campaigns and voting of different groups, the relationships of social and personal characteristics to the candidate choices of voters, and the impact of campaigns on electoral decisions. Gerald M. Pomper, **Elections in America** (Dodd, Mead, 1968, pb) is a study of the relationship of voting and elections to public policy decision-making. Pomper analyzes the function of elections in a democracy and indicates particular strengths and limitations of the vote as a political resource. The techniques of modern election campaigns and the impact of various types of campaigns on the decisions of voters is the focus of Dan Nimmo, **The Political Persuaders** (Prentice-Hall, 1970, pb). Nimmo discusses the generation and use of campaign research, the tactics of mass persuasion, the impact of the mass media on the electorate, and the development and use of professional campaign management agencies. A brief historical description of presidential elections, from 1789 to 1964, is provided in Eugene H. Roseboom, **A Short History of Presidential Elections** (Collier, 1967, pb).

What are the functions of political parties in the American political system? How are the Democratic and Republican parties organized to carry out particular functions? What forces have influenced the development of the particular structures and functions of political parties in the United States? These questions are discussed extensively in Frank J. Sorauf, **Political Parties in the American System** (Little, Brown, 1964, pb). Leon D. Epstein, **Political Parties in Western Democracies** (Praeger, 1967, pb) examines the development, styles of organization, and functions of political parties in twenty nations. He gives special attention to comparison of political parties in the United States and Great Britain.

Interest Groups and Lobbying

The political activity of interest groups is basic to the functioning of modern democratic societies. Interest groups, in conjunction with political parties, are the primary means outside of public government through which political influence and power are applied to public policy-making. Abraham Holtzman, **Interest Groups and Lobbying** (Macmillan, 1966, pb) is an examination of the organization and functions of interest groups in the United States. For comparative purposes, some attention is given to discussion of interest groups in Great Britain and Italy. The role of lobbyist is studied. Lester Milbrath, **The Washington Lobbyist** (Rand McNally, 1963) is a detailed study of the role behavior of lobbyists to the national government. An excellent study of the influence of interest groups and lobbyists on foreign-trade policymaking is Raymond A. Bauer, Ithiel de Sola Pool, and Lewis A. Dexter, **American Business and Public Policy** (Atherton, 1963). Readers interested in the subject of political radicalism will want to read **Rules for Radicals** (Random House, 1971) by Saul D. Alinsky.

The Roles of Public Officials

The roles and statuses of key public officials and the processes of public policy decision-making are essential categories of political science. The role of the Presidency and the role behavior of recent incumbents is the subject matter of Richard E. Neustadt, **Presidential Power** (Wiley, 1960). A study of the Presidency during the Kennedy Administration is presented in Theodore R. Sorenson, **Decision-Making in the White House** (Columbia Univ., 1963).

The role of Congressman and the legislative process is the focus of John Bibby and Roger Davidson, **On Capitol Hill** (Holt, 1967, pb). The various rights and duties of Congressmen, such as legislator, ombudsman, political educator, legitimator, and overseer of the administration, are analyzed. Social and personal pressures which influence the political behavior of Congressmen and the passage of legislation are presented through several case studies. Lewis A. Dexter, **The Sociology and Politics of Congress** (Rand McNally, 1969) discusses how citizens can affect legislative outcomes and actions through voting and participation in election campaigns and how citizens can influence legislation through interest group activity and lobbying.

The structure and functions of the judiciary, the roles of judges, the judge as policymaker, and the relationship of the court system to the political system and to the socio-cultural context are the subjects of discussion of two studies. They offer new perspectives on the judicial system in the United States. Glendon Schubert, **Judicial Policy-Making** (Scott, Foresman, 1965, pb) and Herbert Jacob, **Justice in America**

(Little, Brown, 1965, pb) demonstrate that judges are policymakers as well as enforcers of norms and interpreters of laws.

To understand modern government, one must understand bureaucracies. Charles E. Jacob, **Policy and Bureaucracy** (Van Nostrand, 1966, pb) is a study of bureaucrats as formulators and executors of public policy decisions. Peter Woll, **American Bureaucracy** (Norton, 1963, pb) is a brief introduction to the organization and functions of bureaucracy in American government. The author studies the relationships of bureaucracy to the courts, the Congress, and the Presidency.

Political Systems

Conceptual frameworks which focus on the relationships of social and political institutions have been devised to structure studies of political systems. For example, John D. Lees, **The Political System of the United States** (Harper & Row, 1969, pb) is an analysis of the relationships of the American political system to the social system within which the political institutions function. Karl W. Deutsch, **Politics and Government** (Houghton Mifflin, 1970, pb) is a comparison of the political systems of five modern countries: the United States, the Soviet Union, the United Kingdom, France, and the German Federal Republic. This comparison of political systems is conducted in terms of conceptual frameworks that are articulated in the first half of the book. Among other components of the conceptual frameworks are socio-cultural factors related to the functioning of political institutions. For example, the author analyzes the relationship of political socialization to the maintenance and change of political systems and the relationship of social stratification systems to variation in the exercise of political influence and power.

Teaching About Politics

What new instructional materials about politics are available to elementary and secondary school teachers? How and what should students learn about politics? Numerous suggestions about what and how to teach about politics are presented in Robert E. Cleary, **Political Education in the American Democracy** (Intext Educational Publishers, 1971, pb). Cleary argues that youngsters should have the opportunity to develop analytic capabilities and knowledge of political affairs through the study of public issues. Fred M. Newmann, **Clarifying Public Controversy** (Little, Brown, 1970) advocates the teaching of critical thinking skills through lessons which assist students to rationally consider conflicting value judgments. New materials available to teachers are reviewed in Mary Jane Turner, **Materials for Civics, Government, and**

Problems of Democracy (SSEC, 1971, pb). Realistic aims for teaching and learning about civics are presented by Charles N. Quigley and R. P. Longaker in **Conflict, Politics and Freedom** (Ginn, 1968, pb). Problems in teaching about politics are discussed in Donald H. Riddle and Robert E. Cleary, eds., **Political Science in the Social Studies** (NCSS, 1966, pb). And for secondary school teachers, supervisors, and trainers there's value in John J. Patrick's **Political Socialization of American Youth: Implications for Secondary School Social Studies,** Research Bulletin 3 (NCSS, 1967); and John J. Patrick and Allen D. Glenn, **The Young Voter** (NCSS, 1972). A bibliography, with many descriptions of useful publications, is provided in **Reading Guide in Politics and Government,** by Robert H. Connery, R. H. Leach, and Joseph Zikmund II, Bulletin 38 (NCSS, 1966).

Teachers should be informed about new developments in political science in order to present the most valid, reliable, and relevant information to students. By acquainting students with up-to-date findings of political scientists and the means for deriving these findings, teachers can introduce students to knowledge and ways of knowing that can enable them to more competently perceive and interpret the political world.

9

Sociology

PAUL E. KELLY

Introduction to Sociology

The usual introduction to sociology is provided by a standard college introductory textbook in the field, supplemented by appropriate classroom lectures and discussion and by supplementary readings. **Books in Print** (Bowker) includes library lists of a fairly wide selection of introductory textbooks in sociology, and there is little agreement among sociologists on which of these books is best. Any recently published college-level beginning textbook in sociology of a major publisher may be acceptable. For a number of years, the best seller among these has been Leonard Broom and Philip Selznick, **Sociology: A Text With Adapted Readings** (Harper & Row, 1968). The Sociological Resources for the Social Studies Project of the American Sociological Association, financed by a grant from the National Science Foundation, has produced an innovative new course utilizing the inquiry method, **Inquiries in Sociology** (Allyn & Bacon, 1972), recommended for secondary school use, but useful in introducing sociology at any level. This course can be supplemented by units called "episodes" and paperback readers from the same project and publisher. This basic textbook was initially developed by Everett K. Wilson. Independently, he authored a somewhat more conventional college introductory textbook, **Sociology: Rules, Roles, and Relationships** (Dorsey, 1971). Among the conventional college introduc-

---

Paul E. Kelly is Associate Head, Department of Sociology and Anthropology, University of Georgia, Athens, Georgia.

tory textbooks in sociology, one of the more sophisticated, but now somewhat dated, books is Harry M. Johnson, **Sociology: A Systematic Introduction** (Harcourt, 1960).

Paperback study guides such as Alfred M. Lee, ed., **Principles of Sociology** (Barnes and Noble, 1969, pb) are designed primarily for use in conjunction with standard textbooks, and thus have limited use. George Simpson, **Man in Society: Preface to Sociology and the Social Sciences** (Random House, 1954, pb) and Caroline B. Rose, **Sociology: The Study of Man in Society** (Merrill, 1965, pb) are brief and simple introductions to sociology. Ely Chinoy, **Sociological Perspective** (Random House, 1967, pb), which emphasizes a conceptual approach, is slightly more advanced, and Scott G. McNall, **The Sociological Experience: A Modern Introduction to Sociology** (Little, Brown, 1969, pb) is really a paperback introductory textbook. When used in conjunction with Scott G. McNall, **The Sociological Perspective: Introductory Readings** (Little, Brown, 1968, pb), a reasonably comprehensive coverage is provided. Other introductory level paperbacks of note include Peter L. Berger, **Invitation to Sociology: A Humanistic Perspective** (Doubleday, 1963, pb), which is a good book for the educated non-specialist, particularly the first 121 pages, which are written in a charming style; the treatment, however, is personal and somewhat unconventional. Alex Inkeles, **What Is Sociology? An Introduction to the Discipline and Profession** (Prentice-Hall, 1965, pb) attempts to define sociology and to outline its principal subject matter. Alan P. Bates, **The Sociological Enterprise** (Houghton Mifflin, 1967, pb) and Raymond W. Mack, **A Career in Sociology** (American Sociological Assn., 1967, pb) consider sociology as a career. Roscoe C. Hinkle, Jr., and Gisela J. Hinkle, **The Development of Modern Sociology** (Random House, 1954, pb) is a short history of sociology in the United States, and Charles H. Page, ed., **Sociology and Contemporary Education** (Random House, 1963, pb) attempts to put sociology in perspective as a current educational enterprise.

Details of Basic Sociology

To understand sociology, it is necessary to understand both the elements of sociological theory and the elements of social research. An introduction to the former is provided by Robert K. Merton, **Social Theory and Social Structure** (Free Press, 1957), which goes beyond the introductory text and has become a standard reference. A recent book of Lewis A. Coser, **Masters of Sociological Theory: Ideas in Historical and Social Context** (Harcourt, 1971), considers principal social theorists in historical context, meeting the needs for a beginning reference work.

Hubert M. Blalock, Jr., **An Introduction to Social Research** (Prentice-Hall, 1970, pb) and Sanford Labovitz and Robert Hagedorn, **Introduction to social Research** (McGraw-Hill, 1971, pb) appear to be among the best elementary introductions to social research. Beyond these, there are, of course, a number of standard research methods textbooks used in the methods courses; but they are meant to be used in conjunction with expert instruction and supervised projects. A number of paperback readers are designed to be used to supplement introductory textbooks and give some appreciation of the nature of sociological research. Phillip E. Hammond, ed., **Sociologists at Work: Essays on the Craft of Social Research** (Basic Books, 1964, pb) gives insight into the research process.

In the general field there are a number of standard references, including specialized sociological dictionaries, of which an inexpensive one is Henry P. Fairchild, **Dictionary of Sociology and Related Sciences** (Littlefield, Adams, 1961, pb). It should be kept in mind that there is lack of agreement on the definition of many terms. A handy reference work is Robert E. L. Faris, ed., **Handbook of Modern Sociology** (Rand McNally, 1964). Sociological and other sources are dealt with in the **International Encyclopedia of the Social Sciences** (Macmillan, 1968).

Special Areas of Sociology

Chapters by acknowledged experts in each of the major areas of sociology are included in Robert K. Merton, Leonard Broom, and Leonard S. Cottrell, Jr., eds., **Sociology Today: Problems and Prospects** (Basic Books, 1959), a volume commissioned by and completed under the auspices of the American Sociological Association, the organization from which copies are available. This book is a standard reference.

The second course in sociology is often a course on the family. It is also a course frequently offered at the secondary-school level. Judson T. Landis and Mary G. Landis, **Personal Adjustment, Marriage, and Family Living** (Prentice-Hall, 1970), a practical guide, is typical of the books used for such a course at the secondary-school level. This book provides the secondary-school version of their college textbook, **Building a Successful Marriage** (Prentice-Hall, 1968). As its title suggests, it emphasizes a practical approach to the problems of marriage and family living. Other standard works in the field include: Robert O. Blood, Jr., **Marriage** (Free Press, 1969), William M. Kephart, **The Family, Society, and the Individual** (Houghton Mifflin, 1972), J. Richard Udry, **The Social Context of Marriage** (Lippincott, 1971), and Robert F. Winch, **The Modern Family** (Holt, 1971).

Another basic course in sociology usually concentrates on major American social problems, including poverty, race relations, juvenile delinquency and crime, and various forms of deviance. Sometimes the introductory course emphasizes the problems approach, but this is not the generally preferred approach in the beginning course, where it is felt that normal rather than abnormal human relations ought to receive emphasis. A good book on American society which does not emphasize a problems approach is Robin M. Williams, Jr., **American Society: A Sociological Interpretation** (Knopf, 1970), an especially good volume for American history teachers who wish to incorporate relevant sociological material in their history courses. A worthwhile paperback emphasizing social change in American society is Raymond W. Mack, **Transforming America: Patterns of Social Change** (Random House, 1967, pb). Standard textbooks for a course in social problems, which ordinarily presuppose an introductory course, are: Howard S. Becker, ed., **Social Problems: A Modern Approach** (Wiley, 1966), Robert A. Dentler, **Major American Social Problems** (Rand McNally, 1967), Russell R. Dynes and others, **Social Problems: Dissensus and Deviation in an Industrial Society** (Oxford Univ., 1964), Paul B. Horton and Gerald R. Leslie, **The Sociology of Social Problems** (Appleton-Century-Crofts, 1970), and J. Alan Winter, Jerome Rabow, and Mark Chesler, eds., **Vital Problems for American Society: Meanings and Means** (Random House, 1968). Many paperback books are available but vary in worth on specialized topics within the social problems area. Some are sociologically sound and some are not. The reputation of the author is perhaps the best guide to selection. A good, but dated, book, which may be taken as an example, is Arnold Rose, **The Negro in America** (Harper, 1948, pb), the approved condensed version of Gunnar Myrdal's monumental **An American Dilemma** (Harper, 1944), still, more than a quarter century after its publication, the starting place for any serious consideration of the problem of the Negro in America. It needs, of course, to be supplemented by more recent works.

Teaching Sociology

There is a growing interest in improving the teaching of sociology, particularly at the secondary-school level. The Sociological Resources for the Social Studies Project of the American Sociological Association has produced materials (Allyn & Bacon) specifically for use at this level. A teaching methods book written primarily from a sociological point of view is Earl S. Johnson, **Theory and Practice of the Social Studies** (Macmillan, 1956). Rose's introductory booklet mentioned early in this chapter includes a section on teaching sociology. Useful articles appear from time to time in *Social Education,* the official journal of the National Council for the Social Studies.

PART TWO

Societal Problems and Issues

10

Societal Problems

JONATHON C. McLENDON and IRVING MORRISSETT

Recognition of societal problems has only recently begun to gain the serious attention of a majority of students, teachers, and social scientists. The past half century has found an increasingly strong focus on such problems in social studies curricula in schools and colleges. However, advancement has come mostly through some of the social sciences — history, geography, and political science (government) — areas which flowered in the 1950's and in the first half of the 1960's. The other overlooked social science disciplines gained some acceptances for courses, though the social studies curriculum was not extensive enough to make room for all of these specialized fields. By late if not the mid-1960's there were requests and even demands that recognition be given to the study of highly important societal problems.

The first section in this chapter suggests publications dealing broadly with societal problems. The next section points out publications focusing on some limited societal problems; however, these volumes relate such problems to social studies teaching. The third section notes curricular changes in social science/social studies that were attempted during the 1960's. The last section recommends a few publications on research involving social science/social studies (both disciplines and societal problems).

Jonathon McLendon is Professor of Social Studies, College of Education, University of Georgia, Athens, Georgia. Irving Morrissett is Executive Director, Social Science Education Consortium, Boulder, Colorado, and Professor of Economics, University of Colorado.

Overviews of Societal Problems

Leading guides of a generation ago reflect a national commission's concern for social science/social studies. More than 16 volumes were produced, reporting the status of social science/social studies and indicating needed improvements in social education. Several of these volumes reflect the changes attempted in the teaching of social studies. A small book, **Discussion of Human Affairs: An Inquiry into the Nature of the Statements. . . .** (Macmillan, 1936), was prepared by Charles A. Beard, leader of this major national commission. Beard presented clearly and practically the actions essential to improvement. A more recent overview of changing disciplines and society appears in Kenneth E. Boulding, **Impact of the Social Sciences** (Rutgers Univ., 1966). Donald W. Calhoun in a recent book, **Social Sciences in an Age of Change** (Free Press, 1971), reflects still changing social science disciplines, but definitely indicates the rapidly growing shift toward societal problems from, as well as beyond, social sciences. Perhaps the shift is even more evident in **Education and Social Problems** by Carl Weinberg (Free Press, 1971). In a collection of essays and addresses, Judson R. Landis, ed., sets forth **Current Perspectives on Social Problems** (Wadsworth Publishing Co., Inc., 1969, pb).

Outstanding earlier works include Stuart Chase's **Study of Mankind** (Harper, 1963, pb); its first edition was published in 1948. Many of Chase's books sold well to the public, and it was he who called attention to the dominance of separate disciplines, now shifted into societal and individual problems.

Limited Societal Problems

Numerous chapters or sections discussing societal problems appear in some important social studies books that deal also with social science disciplines. Three books of useful readings are: Mark Krug and others, eds., **The New Social Studies;** Byron Massialas and Andreas Kazamias, eds., **Crucial Issues in the Teaching of Social Studies;** and Irving Morrissett and W. W. Stevens, Jr., eds., **Social Science in the Schools.** Similarly, a number of social problems are analyzed in Vincent R. Rogers, ed., **A Sourcebook for Social Studies** (Macmillan, 1969, pb). A compilation for teachers that includes some variety of social problems is Leonard S. Kenworthy, **Background Papers for Social Studies Teachers** (Wadsworth, 1966, pb).

Especially for social studies teachers are some of the societal problems that are discussed in Peter R. Senn, **Social Science and Its Methods** (Holbook, 1971, pb). Increasingly, textbooks for social studies teachers that analyze subjects, content, structure, and/or social sciences tend toward instruction in the field of societal problems. Perhaps this trend is evident in J. C. McLendon, ed., **Social Science Disciplines: Fundamental for Curriculum Development** (Univ. of Georgia, 1971), where chapters on disciplines conclude with a longer chapter presenting at least three societal problems for curriculum.

Curricular Changes

While nationally recognized social science/social studies projects, institutes, and centers mostly stressed new approaches to courses in the disciplines, the latter part of the 1960's found shifts to societal problems. Proposals during this decade sometimes dealt with theories of particular instructional methods, but some key publications included parts of general social studies curriculum. Representative is G. Wesley Soward, **Social Studies: Curriculum Proposals for the Future** (Scott, Foresman, 1963), which reported an important conference at Stanford University. Many leaders directed social studies toward the study of societal problems, especially by publication of their findings. An example of this, with alternatives plus curriculum directions, is **Social Studies in Transition: Guidelines for Change** (NCSS, 1966), edited by Dorothy M. Fraser and S. P. McCutchen.

Curriculum development proposals for a decade were set forth at NCSS annual meetings and committee sessions. Follow-up and development came with the publication of the NCSS yearbook of 1969 on curriculum. Co-authors Frederick R. Smith and C. Benjamin Cox dealt mainly with organization in **New Strategies and Curriculum in Social Studies** (Rand McNally, 1969, pb). Some curriculum, instruction, materials, and publications on social science did stress "what" as well as "how" to teach. Emphasis on this was apparent in G. W. Ford and Lawrence Pugno, eds., **Structure of Knowledge and the Curriculum** (Rand McNally, 1964, pb).

Possibly most exciting to numerous readers was John S. Gibson, **New Frontiers in the Social Studies** (Citation, 1965, pb). Gibson clearly and briefly set forth changes in school curriculums and reported mid-Sixties' materials for social studies. Somewhat comparable is a collection of articles edited by Byron G. Massialas and F. R. Smith, **New Challenges in the Social Studies** (Wadsworth, 1965, pb). The book reported some types and results of research, including approaches to social studies teaching and curriculum. Somewhat broader readings for teachers are presented in James P. Shaver and Harold Berlak, eds., **Democracy, Pluralism and the Social Studies** (Houghton Mifflin, 1968, pb). More devoted to current problems is Richard E. Gross and Raymond H. Muessig, eds., **Problem-Centered Social Studies Instruction** (NCSS, 1971, pb). Distinctive chapters set forth elementary, junior high, and senior high levels of guidance toward reflective teaching, and there is considerable material for use of teachers.

Social Science/Social Studies Educational Research

A few publications of value to teachers discuss a wide range of matters, from issues on social studies to various social sciences, and some include research on societal problems. The latter, for example, is reflected in Bernard Berelson's edition of twenty papers on **Behavioral Sciences Today** (Basic, 1963, pb). Other articles appear in Daniel Lerner, ed., **Human Meanings and the Social Sciences** (Meridian, 1959, pb), a very readable volume.

Desirable examples of research books include: John Madge, **Tools of the Social Sciences** (Anchor, 1965, pb); Robert R. Brown, **Explanation in Social Sciences** (Aldine, 1963, pb); Maurice Duverger, **An Introduction to the Social Sciences** (Praeger, 1964); and Donald P. Ray, ed., **Trends in Social Science** (Philosophical Library, 1961).

Few publications to date use the word "research" in their titles, for it has traditionally and widely been considered that teachers do not want such material. Attempting to present an easily readable, brief report is Jonathon C. McLendon and F.C. Penix, **What Research Says to the Teacher: Teaching the Social Studies** (NEA, 1968, pb). With a greater scope is Ronald Lippitt and others, **Teachers' Role in Social Science Investigation** (Research Assn., 1969, pb). The largest volume for teachers (including secondary school teachers, despite its title) is Wayne L. Herman, **Current Research in Elementary School Social Studies** (Macmillan, 1969, pb). Many articles can provide useful information for social studies teachers. The scope and financing of social studies research are regrettably not as extensive as they should be. One work that shows the value of such support is J. B. Sanders, **Social Science Requirements for Bachelor's Degrees Nationwide** (USHEW, 1959, pb). Fortunately, at least some state or local agencies report social studies data of interest to many employed in this field.

11

Citizenship and Human Rights

JOHN S. GIBSON

It is the essence of democracy that the people decide; it is the peril of democracy when they do so in ignorance. Citizenship education continues to emphasize the need for enlightened and effective participants in a democratic civic culture irrespective of changes in styles of participation and the nature of the civic culture itself. Studies in recent years have shed much light on how the learner is oriented into the realm of politics and governance, or political socialization; the impact of the school in citizenship education; and promising practices in this area for teachers and students.

Before reviewing these three areas of citizenship education, note should be taken of Gabriel Almond and Sidney Verba's **The Civic Culture** (Little, Brown, 1965, pb), which presents a comparison of the democratic civic cultures of the United States, Great Britain, Italy, Germany, and Mexico. This book affords the reader an excellent conceptualization of patterns of citizenship participation in a democratic civic culture.

Citizenship

Political socialization is considered in Chapter 8 in this Bulletin, and Fred I. Greenstein's **Children and Politics** (Yale Univ., 1965, pb) has become a classic in appraising how children acquire political values and attitudes. **Development of Political Attitudes in Children** by Robert D.

John S. Gibson is Director, Lincoln Filene Center for Citizenship and Public Affairs, Tufts University, Medford, Massachusetts.

Hess and Judith V. Torney (Aldine, 1967, pb) is another major contribution in the area of political or civic development. These works, along with John S. Gibson's **Citizenship** (Dimension, 1968, pb), agree that the child develops his or her basic orientation toward the civic culture between very early years and about age 13. This orientation includes attitudes toward such authoritative figures as parents, the President, police, laws; feelings about political efficacy or alienation; and a positive identification with one's nation.

Studies of recent years report unfavorable news in general concerning the role of the schools in providing effective and stimulating civic education, especially at the high school level. One has only to read the article by Kenneth P. Langton and M. Kent Jennings in a 1968 issue of *American Political Science Review*. Or John Patrick's study, **Political Socialization of American Youth: Implications for Secondary Social Studies** (NCSS, 1967, pb), which also indicates that most high school courses in civics and related subjects, as presently taught, have little or no relevancy to the civic understanding or commitment of high school students in the political cultures in which they live. There is too much concentration on textbooks, lectures, and other cognitive approaches to an area so immersed in values, attitudes, emotions, and sensitivities. Further, the real world of politics and government is often missing in school programs, as these studies note. Patrick points out that:

> In the absence of out-of-school political experiences, it is doubtful that the typical twelfth-grader has a vastly more profound understanding of the political system and political behavior than the typical ninth- or tenth-grader.

In brief, there is much evidence to support the position that effective and relevant civic education is a clear and pressing need, not only in the social studies but also in all areas of school life.

Analyses of prospective activities in teaching have appeared recently. Gibson catalogued the deficiencies of civic education and called for major surgery in a 1969 issue of *Bulletin of the National Association of Secondary School Principals*. Donald W. Robinson, Elmer Pflieger, Harold Oyer, and Daniel Roselle reviewed the curricular and co-curricular programs of many high schools in the United States in order to identify outstanding efforts to make citizenship education relevant and significant to students. Their book, **Promising Practices in Civic Education** (NCSS, 1967, pb), is an excellent handbook for schools and teachers seeking to improve their programs in this area.

Because the discipline of political science is so essential to school programs in civic education, the 36th NCSS Yearbook did educators a great service in presenting the many facets of political science and in treating their relevance to the curriculum. Mary Jane Turner's **Materials for Civics, Government, and Problems of Democracy** (Social Science Education Consortium, 1971) is most helpful in describing programs in progress throughout the United States that, through instructional resources and other means, can help any school to increase the effectiveness and quality of its citizenship education programs. Some people disapprove of its traditional emphasis, but the Joy Elmer Morgan collection of **The American Citizens Handbook** (NCSS, 1968) continues to sell to quite a number of readers.

Human Rights

The 1948 United Nations Declaration of Human Rights still remains as the shining document expressing the fundamental rights of man (and woman!), and we should continually return to the Declaration for inspiration and hope. The security, dignity, and well-being of the individual can be approached by re-examining the meaning and vitality of the American Bill of Rights. Irving Brant provides historical and contemporary perspective in this respect in **The Bill of Rights: Its Origin and Meaning** (Mentor, 1967, pb), as he traces the evolution of these basic rights and how they were interpreted by the Supreme Court of the late 1960's. Alan Barth also provides a refreshing appraisal of the rights in "Contemporary Meaning of the Bill of Rights" in the NCSS 36th Yearbook. Paul D. Hines and Leslie Wood, **A Guide to Human Rights Education** (NCSS, 1969, pb) is directly and particularly concerned with teaching social studies. Human rights within the context of our nation's judicial and governing system receive careful and sensitive treatment by Paul A. Freund in his study entitled **On Law and Justice** (Harvard Univ., 1968). There are many other general works on the nature and meaning of human rights; however, some areas of particular significance today are the struggle for rights by minority groups, the issue of civil disobedience and nonviolence, and the role of the courts. Some outstanding textbooks in this field can also be identified.

The life and struggles of Martin Luther King, Jr., symbolize the long uphill road travelled by so many people in the quest for equality. Ed Clayton's **Martin Luther King: The Peaceful Warrior** (Prentice-Hall, 1968, pb) and Dolores Harrison's **We Shall Live in Peace: The Teachings of Martin Luther King, Jr.** (Hawthorn, 1968) merit our close attention. A broader discussion of the black American's struggle to achieve freedom and first-class citizenship may be found in Janet Harris' **Long Freedom Road** (McGraw-Hill, 1967). Frances Cavanah's **Our Country's Freedom** (Rand McNally, 1966) traces the efforts of many minority groups to achieve essential constitutional freedoms.

Dr. King, of course, had much to say and did much in the area of "positive" civil disobedience and nonviolent approaches toward achieving basic rights. These are powerful themes and should be an integral part of any social studies curriculum. Staughton Lynd gives us a heady background study in his **Nonviolence in America: A Documentary His-**

tory (Bobbs-Merrill, 1966, pb). Laurence Veysey's **Law and Resistance: American Attitudes Toward Authority** (Harper & Row, 1970, pb), a splendid book of readings, deals with the nature and limits of authority, patterns of confrontation outside the law, and the police as a contemporary symbol of authority. Former Supreme Court Justice Abe Fortas provides a learned and eminently readable overview in **Concerning Dissent and Civil Disobedience** (Signet, 1968, pb). Finally, let us not consider Thoreau irrelevant to the 1970's.

In these turbulent days, many are reviewing the role of the courts with respect to sustaining and strengthening human rights. Although it has been around for many years, Anthony Lewis' **Gideon's Trumpet** (Random House, 1964, pb) still remains as an outstanding treatment of the nation's courts and the judicial process in the realm of a very essential right: access to counsel. **Civil Rights, the Constitution, and the Court** by Archibald Cox, deWolfe, and Wiggins (Harvard Univ., 1967) is a superb analysis of the interactions between the courts and human rights. Civil liberties for adolescents are also an area to which social studies teachers should give more attention, and W. E. Cavenagh's **Juvenile Court: The Child and the Law** (Penguin, 1967) admirably meets this need. Another work in this important area is John Paul Hanna's **Teenagers and the Law** (Ginn, 1967, pb).

Three textbooks deserve particular attention because they are most enlightening for the teacher and because they are outstanding vehicles for dealing with human rights in the classroom. William M. Gibson's **Lessons in Conflict: Legal Education Materials for Secondary Schools** (Lincoln Filene Center, 1971) treats many dimensions of law that affect the rights and responsibilities of young people, while Donald Parker, O'Neil, and Econopouly's **Civil Liberties: Case Studies and the Law** (Houghton Mifflin, 1965, pb) zeroes in on the specific rights of young and old alike. Finally, **The Pursuit of Justice** by Henry W. Bragdon and John C. Pittenger (Macmillan, 1969) presents case studies for each right within the context of American history and contemporary events. U.S. citizenship and comparative Russian aims are presented in Dale L. Brubaker's **Alternative Directions for the Social Studies** (International, 1967, pb).

12

Current Events

PHILMORE B. WASS

The ultimate goal of all social studies instruction is to provide young people with the basic understandings and skills essential to enable them to make sense out of life. If this goal is achieved youth will be able to relate constructively to other people, and to their society. Failure to achieve this goal may result in a dangerous degree of alienation. Since the voting age has been lowered to eighteen, the study of current issues has assumed even greater importance because a knowledge of current events and the acquisition of related skills are the bases upon which constructive civic participation must be built.

In spite of the obvious need for current affairs instruction, the literature of the social studies is almost bare of books in this field. Lillian Howitt, **Enriching the Curriculum with Current Events** (Aldine, 1964, pb) is well described by its title. It should be especially helpful at the junior high level.

Of interest is "Seven Polarizing Issues in America Today," in **Annals of the American Academy of Political & Social Science** (AAPSS, 1971). This excellent publication provides background for teaching about many of the current issues which frequently appear in the news. The topics considered are military withdrawal from abroad, effective crackdown on crime, federal revenue on localities and states, President versus congressional power, enfranchising youth, pornography regulated, and women's liberation. Two authors tackle each issue, expressing not necessarily opposing points of view but rather unique outlooks in a scholarly manner.

Philmore B. Wass is Professor, School of Education, and Director, Center for Economic Education, University of Connecticut, Storrs, Connecticut. Assisting were Bernard Marlin and William Morrison.

To understand the issues of today it is important to know of the issues of earlier periods. John Brooks, **The Great Leap: The Past Twenty-Five Years in America** (Harper & Row, 1966, pb) provides a valuable and intellectually stimulating picture of our nation during the last quarter of a century. The author believes 1939 to be a watershed year in American history. It marked the end of the Great Depression and the beginning of our worldwide involvement in a war which was already scarring the face of Europe. Margaret Mead stated that the changes occurring in this period of twenty-five years (1939-1964) were as deep as the changes separating Stone Age men from the builders of cities. The recent marked alterations in the American character, which have to be the central factor in any study of public issues, are clearly delineated by John Brooks.

Current Affairs Pamphlets

Fortunately, contrasted with the paucity of books on techniques for teaching current affairs, there is a wealth of student materials in this field. Most extensive pamphlets dealing with national issues are **Public Affairs Pamphlets** semi-monthly (Public Affairs Committee) and **AEP Unit Books: Public Issues Series** pamphlets (American Education Publications).

The Center for Information on America (Washington, Connecticut) publishes **Vital Issues.** These are four-page pamphlets which come out ten times per year covering a wide range of topics. In addition, the Center publishes **Grass Roots Guides on Democracy and Practical Politics.**

In foreign affairs, the **Headline Series** (Foreign Policy Assn.) is well known and widely used. For those interested in a different point of view on international problems, the Atlantic Information Centre for Teachers (London) publishes a series called **Crisis Papers** issued six times a year. The Centre publishes other materials including **The World and the School,** which is issued three times a year. This publication includes bibliographies and suggestions on teaching and social studies curriculum development. Write for descriptive materials published by the Centre.

School Periodicals and Newspapers

Two major publishing organizations now offer weekly news periodicals designed for student use: American Education Publications and Scholastic Magazines. Both companies publish a variety of periodicals. Weekly papers start AEP primary grades, while Scholastic covers the middle grades. Both companies offer sample sets of their materials.

New York Times offers special news materials for students. *Student*

Weekly is a newspaper of twelve pages prepared for senior high students. In addition *New York Times* issues extensive multi-media current affairs materials, including monthly filmstrips with accompanying records, special sets of filmstrips on problem areas; for example, **Cities: People and Their Problems.** Audio cassettes are also published on which *New York Times* staff discuss major national and international problems.

The Christian Science Monitor reprints many of its major series on vital current topics. These are available from University Microfilms (Xerox). Other major weekly news magazines also publish editions with accompanying suggestions for pupil use. For materials on the use of newspapers in the classroom, the best source seems to be the American Newspaper Publishers Association Foundation. The following pamphlets can be obtained: **Daily Newspaper in the School Curriculum; Teacher and the Newspaper; Two Week Teaching Unit for Elementary Grades; How to Get More Out of Your Newspaper; Remedial Reading and the Newspaper.** Nearly all of these guides were prepared by teachers, drawing upon their classroom experiences.

"Newspaper-in-the-Classroom" summer workshops are another major service sponsored by the ANPA in cooperation with newspapers in three regions. Inquiries on the location of these workshops should be addressed to ANPA or the co-sponsoring National Council for the Social Studies. Most local newspapers, which carry on "Newspaper-in-the-Classroom" programs, make copies available for school use at reduced cost.

Several companies are now producing various types of audio-visual materials for the study of current affairs. For example, Denoyer-Geppert Audio-Visuals has produced a series of sound filmstrips dealing with a wide range of issues. Guidance Associates yields a series of sound filmstrips on **Contemporary Social Issues.** The Center for Cassette Studies is producing cassette tapes featuring outstanding leaders in various fields speaking on major problems, both national and international.

Current Events and the Future

Presumably studying both history and current affairs insures that the wisest possible decisions are made for the future. Yet often the future implications of issues and policies are not explored. Scholars in many fields are now paying increased attention to a study of the future. This realization makes it imperative that the long-range impact of all decisions be carefully evaluated. The necessity of preparing young people to cope with future change is the subject of a widely read book by Alvin Toffler, **Future Shock** (Random House, 1970, pb). Surveying a host of imminent changes that seem to be overriding our values and institutions, Toffler shows how "future shock" like cultural lag results when there is a limited human response to the rapid pace of change.

In **Technological Man: The Myth and the Reality** (Braziller, 1969, pb) Victor Ferkiss has developed a qualified but more encouraging view of the future relationships between man, society and burgeoning technology. The great need at this time, according to Ferkiss, is a new philosophy to guide this new type man to maturation. A highly scholarly presentation on the future is "Toward the Year 2000" in the journal *Daedalus* (American Academy of Arts and Sciences, 1967). A commission prepared statements that the future begins in the present, and gave careful consideration to future consequences of decisions. With such authorities as Daniel Bell, Erik Erikson, and Margaret Mead as contributors to this volume, teachers are assured of a valuable resource for teaching about the future.

Here Comes Tomorrow: Living and Working in the Year 2000, Staff of the *Wall Street Journal* (Dow Jones, 1967, pb), deals with future projections of population growth, transportation, food, urban growth, and other questions which compose the current issues of today. The book is simply written and could be useful to students as well as to teachers.

Stuart Chase, **The Most Probable World** (Harper & Row, 1968, pb) also attempts to point out the directions in which we are heading. He too is aware of the rapid changes being produced by technology, stating that changes are occurring in such rapid succession that one must "write as he runs." In this highly readable and exciting book, the author describes ten current trends and attempts to project them to the year 2000.

13

Social Foundations of Education

NICHOLAS V. COSTANTINO

The severe erosion of the working consensus between students and educators has attracted the attention and efforts of increasing numbers of social scientists whose judgments and research are now precipitating educational events which touch the daily lives of all students. This condition highlights the importance of the social sciences in school curriculums and points to a need for systematic effort directed toward helping students use their knowledge of the social sciences to account for what is happening to and around them in their educational world. Scarcity of factual data, which is both understandable and usable by students, may account for the absence of tested curriculum experiences in this area. Therefore, the selection and organization of the following listed sources suggests both the materials and a model for a social studies unit on education. While many, if not most, sources listed in this guide contain implications for education, only those sources which are clearly identifiable with dominating concepts associated with reading guide chapter headings will be listed by author, chapter, or both. Those with a direct, immediate, and positive relationship to education will be referred to by author, title, publisher, and, where appropriate, chapter.

Nicholas V. Costantino is Assistant Professor, Foundations of Education, College of Education, University of Georgia, Athens, Georgia.

Historical Antecedents

In the study of education, its history functions to provide a comparative basis for evaluating prevailing ideas, conditions and events. Along this line, the historical record of popular education as an article of American faith can be found in Henry Perkinson's **The Imperfect Panacea** (Random House, 1968, pb) and Lawrence A. Cremin's **The Genius of Americian Education** (Random House, 1968, pb). Data on educational thought, growth, support, control, practice, curriculums, and standards can be taken from Newton Edwards and Herman G. Ritchey's **The School in the American Social Order** (Houghton Mifflin, 1963), Ernest E. Bayles and Bruce L. Hood's **Growth of American Educational Thought and Practice** (Harper & Row, 1966), and Robert Potter's **The Stream of American Education** (American, 1967).

For historical perspectives of federal activities in education see Sidney Teidt's **The Role of the Federal Government in Education** (Oxford Univ., 1966) and Sheldon P. Stoff's, **Two-Way Street: A History of Main Trends in School Desegregation in the United States** (David-Stewart, 1967). A well-documented example of the pervasive effects of cultural values on educational policy and practice is available in Raymond E. Callahan's study of the impact of scientific management on public school administration reported in **Education and the Cult of Efficiency** (Univ. of Chicago, 1962, pb). Finally, a convenient survey of changing views of the nature and function of education through the ages may be found in education sections of standard collections of famous quotations.

Contemporary Educational Thought

A plurality of ideologies guide and justify educational policy, practice, and curriculum decisions in the American educational enterprise. Most prevailing views have been catalogued, explained and criticized by John Wynne in **Theories of Education** (Harper & Row, 1963). To complete this picture, see also **Existentialism in Education** (Harper & Row, 1966, pb) by Van Cleve Morris. Major dysfunctions which occur when conflicting theories of education are used to originate, justify and implement policy and practice are delineated and discussed in Henry Ehlers and Gordon C. Lee's **Crucial Issues in Education** (Holt, Rinehart and Winston, 1964). For a sample of contemporary ideas of the "good" which compete in the educational market place see John Rich, **Humanistic Foundations of Education** (Jones, 1971), Paul A. Goodman, **Compulsory Miseducation** (Horizon, 1964, Random, pb), Theodore Schultz, **The Economic Value of Education** (Columbia Univ., 1963), and **The Christian Idea of an Education** (Yale Univ., 1957), Edmund Fuller, ed. Finally, for comparative purposes see **American Education in Foreign Perspectives** (Wiley, 1969), Stewart Fraser, ed.

Political and Economic Aspects

Working consensuses on questions of educational support, control, equality of educational opportunity, and the separation of church and state in education are products of political processes and court actions. Ralph B. Kimbrough's **Political Power and Educational Decision-Making** (Rand McNally, 1964) brings the grass-roots picture into focus. The general case against local control of public education may be found in Myron Lieberman's **The Future of Education** (Univ. of Chicago, 1960). Principles delineating the relationships between church and state are inventoried and explained by Sam Duker in **The Public Schools and Religion** (Harper & Row, 1966). Finally, authoritative but partisan statements in the same area can be found in Paul Blanshard's **Religion and the Public Schools** (Beacon, 1963) and John C. Murray's **We Hold These Truths** (Doubleday, 1964, pb).

The ways in which people make their living in a free and open society have profound effects upon education. A conception of education as a process of developing human resources and a vital means of improving the general welfare through creation of new wealth is exemplified as national policy in the **Economic Report of the President,** Office of the President (USGPO, 1965). This policy has reinforced the prevailing influence of vocationalism in education. Some ill effects of overreacting to this vocationalism have been catalogued and discussed by Ivar Berg in **Education and Jobs: The Great Training Robbery** (Praeger, 1970). For evaluation of the educational implications of current economic thought systems consult **Revolution, Evolution and the Economic Order** (Prentice-Hall, 1962) by Allan W. Sievers. Direct effects of low income upon educational aspirations and achievement have been documented and reported by Pat Sexton in **Education and Income** (Viking, 1961). Finally, see Jerry Miner, **Social and Economic Factors in Spending for Public Education** (Syracuse Univ., 1963, pb) for an in-depth study of the social and economic premises which are used to determine and to justify allocation of the community's resources for education.

Schooling and Sociological Aspects

The school as the locus of social as well as educational forces deserves special emphasis and study. A global picture of the school and the educational process is provided by Jean Grambs' **Schools, Scholars and Society** (Prentice-Hall, 1965, pb). Results of a microscopic examination of the school are set forth in **Growing Up in River City** (Wiley, 1962, pb) by Robert Havighurst and others. An assessment of the efficiency of the school in equalizing educational opportunity is presented in James S. Coleman's "Summary Report," **Equality of Educational Opportunity** (HEW, 1964). Jerome Bruner explores the problem of handling the knowledge explosion in **The Process of Education** (Harvard Univ., 1960, pb). Critical discussions of the purposes, methods, and the results of schooling can be found in Jules Henry's **Culture Against Man** (Random House, 1965), James D. Koerner's **The Case for Basic Education** (Little, Brown, 1959), H. G. Rickover's **American Education: A National Failure** (Dutton, 1963), Charles E. Silberman's **Crisis in the Classroom** (Random House, 1970), **The Experience of Schooling** (Holt, 1971) by Melvin L. Silberman, and **Deschooling Society** (Harper and Row, 1971) by Ivan D. Illich. For the quality of life in the classroom see **Up the Down Staircase** (Avon, 1966, pb) by Bel Kaufman. Finally, for comparative purposes, see **Other Schools and Ours** (Holt, 1967) by Edmund J. King.

The concomitant educational effects of the concentration and homogenization of socially and economically disadvantaged groups in metropolitan aggregates have resulted in the concentration of learning and behavior problems as well as teachers, administrators, and schools. For a survey of these problems see Robert Havighurst and Daniel Levine's **Education in Metropolitan Areas** (Allyn & Bacon, 1971, pb) and James B. Conant's **Slums and Suburbs** (McGraw-Hill, 1961, pb). Studies of some of the deleterious human effects of substandard social environments upon educational aspirations and achievement are available in **Profile of a School Dropout** (Random House, 1968, pb), Daniel Schreiber, ed., **Stability and Change in Human Characteristics** (Wiley, 1964) by Benjamin S. Bloom, and **Education and Social Problems** (Free Press, 1971) by Carl Weinberg. A general idea of the scope and nature of the task of minimizing the deleterious educational effects of early deprivation may be found in **Compensatory Education for Cultural Deprivation** (Holt, 1965, pb) by Benjamin S. Bloom and others.

Finally, for concomitant educational consequences of the emergence of a youth culture with attitudes, beliefs, and values which diverge significantly from those of mature adults, consult the recent statements of Margaret Mead, Erik Ericson, Kenneth Keniston, James S. Coleman, and Edgar Z. Friedenberg. Americans have tended to ascribe an ameliorative function to their educational institutions. Consequently, there always has been a number of visionary educators, education-minded scholars and critics who have bent their efforts to the task of identifying future alternatives in education. In **Education and the New America** (Random House, 1962, pb) Solon T. Kimball and James E. McClellan have explored the educational ramifications of a conception of America as a society that is increasingly characterized by the dominance of the corporation as a social as opposed to a purely economic institution. In a somewhat related effort Burton R. Clark has outlined the educational consequences of the American commitment to technology in **Educating the Expert Society** (Chandler, 1962). Educational prescriptions for attenuating the ill effects of neglecting to recognize that the future has already arrived, engulfed American society, and is levying a prohibitive toll are set forth in Alvin Toffler's **Future Shock** (Random House, 1970). A collection of the products of speculative thinkers on the future dimensions of education can be found in **Designing Education for the Future** (Citation, 1968), Edgar Morphet and David L. Jesser, eds.

14

Environmental Problems and Conservation

ROBERT N. SAVELAND

The ever-burgeoning literature on environmental topics represents a communications explosion of the first magnitude. In order to narrow the field, this reviewer will restrict his references to environmental books of particular interest for social studies teachers.

Problems and Values

To Rachel Carson goes credit for arousing an awareness to environmental problems. Frank Graham, Jr., in **Since Silent Spring** (Houghton Mifflin, 1970, pb), tells the effects of her work. Gene Marine has been called a new breed of muckraker for his **America the Raped: The Engineering Mentality and the Devastation of a Continent** (Avon, 1969, pb). Nevertheless he is persuasive and raises disturbing questions as to whether we need the new jetport, interstate highway, or canal. Helen Leavitt's **Superhighway-Superhoax** (Doubleday, 1970, pb) pursues the special-interest groups affecting governmental policy in road building. George Laycock does a similar job on the Army Corps of Engineers in his **Diligent Destroyers** (Ballantine/National Audubon Society, 1970, pb). **Terracide** (Little, Brown, 1970, pb), by Ron Linton, former official in HEW, gives a frightening account of what could happen here. William H. Whyte stresses the need for planning in **The Last Landscape** (Doubleday, 1970, pb).

America Was Beautiful (Barre, 1969, pb), A. Watson and J. Houston,

Robert N. Saveland is Professor of Social Science Education, University of Georgia, Athens, Georgia.

eds., reproduces engravings of town and country scenes first published by William Cullen Bryant a hundred years ago. Other titles in this geographic area are: Roderick Nash, ed., **American Environment: Readings in the History of Conservation** (Addison-Wesley, 1968, pb); Roger Revelle and Hans H. Lansberg, eds., **America's Changing Environment** (Beacon, 1970, pb); and Sir Frank Fraser Darling and John P. Milton, eds., **Future Environments of North America** (Natural History, 1971, pb).

Among the noted alarm sounders, especially on population problems, has been Paul Ehrlich. Now he has published, with Anne Ehrlich, **Population, Resources, and Environment: Issues in Human Ecology** (Freeman, 1971, pb). The Ehrlichs, like others in the environmental movement, call for a restructuring of values. Social studies teachers especially interested in this topic may also see **Ecological Conscience: Values for Survival** (Prentice-Hall, 1970, pb), edited by Robert Disch.

Five books in the affective domain must be mentioned. In each, the environment underlies a unique social situation. Alfred Slote's **Termination: The Closing of the Baker Plant** (Bobbs-Merrill, 1969, pb) is an authentic and moving study of the human effects of a remote, high-level management decision. In **Will They Ever Finish Bruckner Boulevard?** (Macmillan, 1970, pb), Ada Louise Huxtable tells what urban design is all about. Robert Murphy's **The Stream** (Farrar, 1971, pb) is a novel about the efforts of a ten-man club to keep unspoiled their 2,000 acres in the mountains. In **Inland Island** (Simon & Schuster, 1969, pb), Pulitzer prize-winning author Josephine Johnson tells of her love for the land which she feels "a need to record and cherish and to share. . . ." Oscar Lewis's **A Death in the Sanchez Family** (Random House, 1969, pb) is similar to his earlier works in that the reader experiences the crushing conditions of a Latin American slum through the story of the people.

Teaching and Environment

Certain books can be identified with specific social science disciplines. James L. Green's **Economic Ecology: Baselines for Urban Development** (Univ. of Georgia, 1969, pb) and Marshall Goldman's **Controlling Pollution: The Economics of a Cleaner America** (Prentice-Hall, 1967, pb) develop economic viewpoints. In the realm of political science, James Ridgeway advocates revolutionary changes in his **Politics of Ecology** (Dutton, 1970, pb). Joseph L. Sax recommends a legal approach in his **Defending the Environment: A Strategy for Citizen Action** (Knopf, 1971, pb). Wilbur Zelinsky's **Geography and a Crowding World** (Oxford Univ., 1970, pb) reports on a symposium concerned with population pressures upon physical and social resources in developing lands. A group of graduate students in geography prepared **Congress and the Environment** (Univ. of Washington, 1970, pb) edited by Richard A. Cooley and Geoffrey Wanderforde-Smith. As evidence of the long-term interest of geographers in the environment, **Conservation of Natural Resources,** Guy-Harold Smith, ed. (Wiley, 1971, pb), has appeared in a fourth edition. Special mention should be made of the Commission on College Geography Resource Papers: No. 2 **Air Pollution** and No. 5 **Perception of Environment** (Assn. Amer. Geographers, 1968, 1969, pb).

Environment, Readings for Teachers (Addison-Wesley, 1972, pb), edited by J. W. George Ivany, includes Henning's "Comments on an Interdisciplinary Social Science Approach for Conservation Administration." **The Environmental Problem** (SSEC, 1971, pb), Irving Morrissett and Karen B. Wiley, eds., has selections from House Subcommittee hearings on the Environmental Education Act of 1970. "All Education Is Environmental Education" is the heading on the first page of Mark Terry's **Teaching for Survival: A Handbook for Environmental Education** (Ballantine/Friends of the Earth, 1971, pb). Teachers will find the bibliography of classroom materials to be especially useful. **Outlines of Environmental Education** (Dembar Educational Research Services, 1971, pb), edited by Clay Schoenfeld, is a compendium of articles from the journal, *Environmental Education*. The Association of Classroom Teachers in cooperation with Project Man's Environment of the American Association for Health, Physical Education, and Recreation has published **Man and His Environment: An Introduction to Using Environmental Study Areas** (NEA, 1970, pb). If only one book could be read for general background, teachers have responded more favorably to Raymond F. Dasmann's **Environmental Conservation** (Wiley, 1968, pb).

The series, **People and Their Environment: Teachers' Curriculum Guide to Conservation Education** (Ferguson, 1968, 1969, pb), Matthew J. Brennan, ed., has individual books on the social studies. See also the Task Force on Environment and Natural Resources, **Teachers' Guide for Environmental Education** prepared by the North Carolina State Dept. of Public Instruction (1970, pb). **Environment and the Schools** (National School Public Relations Assn., 1971, pb) describes six state programs and examines some successful local programs. Propriety permits only passing mention of my own **Sourcebooks for World Resources** (Ginn, 1969, 1970, pb), for use by junior and senior high school students.

Handbooks and Readers

The Environmental Handbook (Ballantine, 1970, pb), edited by Garrett de Bell, and **Ecotactics: The Sierra Club Handbook for Environmental Activists** (Pocket, 1970, pb), John G. Mitchell and Constance L. Stallings, eds., are widely available and frequently reviewed. A high-school classroom project that became a magazine and then a book is **The Foxfire Book** (Anchor, 1972, pb), edited by the teacher, Eliot Wigginton. Students sought out longtime residents to learn about mountain skills in using the environment, from quilting to moonshining.

A much discussed book is **The Limits to Growth; A Report for the Club of Rome's Project on the Predicament of Mankind** (Universe, 1972, pb) by Donella H. Meadows, Dennis L. Meadows, Jørgen Randers, and William H. Behrens III. This group sought to utilize a systems approach in evaluating data on divergent parts of world problems. **The Subversive Science** (Houghton Mifflin, 1969, pb), edited by Paul Shepard and Daniel McKinley, and **The Environmental Crisis** (Yale Univ., 1970, pb), edited by Harold W. Helfrich, Jr., also represent scholarly approaches to environmental concerns. Thomas R. Detwyler's **Man's Impact on Environment** (McGraw Hill, 1971, pb), and Paul Ward English and Robert C. Mayfield's **Man, Space, and Environment** (Oxford Univ., 1971, pb) are both used as college textbooks. For the more casual reader they offer the opportunity to use the cafeteria method of reading and therefore should be in the well-stocked environmental library.

Bibliographies

For the reader who wishes a more comprehensive listing than can be provided here, there are several useful bibliographies. Robert W. Durrenberger's **Environment and Man: A Bibliography** (National Press, 1970, pb) is not annotated, but it has a topical classification in the front followed by references to books and articles arranged alphabetically by authors. The "arid zones" listing reflects an interest of the compiler, but there are also extensive references under "man-environment relationships" and "public policies and planning."

More than 100,000 pages were scanned in preparing John A. Moore's **Science for Society: A Bibliography** (American Assn. for the Advancement of Science, 1970, pb). Although not annotated, the listings are arranged by chapters focusing on problems of population, food, pollution, race, aggression, and the quality of life.

The Environmental Crisis: A Paperback Library (Bowker, 1970, pb) has been issued as a reprint from the March 1970 edition of **Paperback Books in Print.** This issue with its annotated bibliography is available in quantity (100 copies @ $12.00 postpaid) and is suitable for classroom use in high schools. Joan Carvajal and Martha Munzer's **Conservation Education: A Selected Bibliography** (Interstate Printers, 1971, pb) has been kept current through the issuing of a supplement. The voluminous **1971 Directory of Environmental Information Sources** (National Foundation for Environmental Control, 1971, pb) includes bibliographic sources, documents, conference proceedings, books, and films dealing with natural resource management, environmental pollution, human ecology, technological assessment, and conservation education. The Educational Research Information Centers (ERIC), especially those in Columbus, Ohio, and Boulder, Colorado, assist in cataloging and disseminating information on environmental curricula and procedures.

15

Humanities

JOHN J. FARRELL

The humanities programs in the elementary-secondary schools are usually derived from basic texts on the subject, which include what one would expect from a smattering of literature, poetry, some lines of music, and bits of art history. This review, however, is primarily concerned with the creation of a humanities program for a specific group, or a general class of varying achievement levels. Each of the sources listed fulfills the prerequisites for the creative teacher—it presents the fundamentals, and also serves as the starting point for tailor-made programs.

Art

For the teacher who is thrust into the role of decision making on values in the fine arts, no volume on the market is more useful than Nathan Knowbler, **The Visual Dialogue** (Holt, 1961); each chapter, by itself, may serve for a week's discussion, and is basic enough to use effectively in instruction. R. L. Gregory, **Eye and Brain, the Psychology of Seeing** (McGraw-Hill, 1966, pb) is an erudite consideration of the physical-mental process of perception; John Canaday, **Keys to Art** (Tudor, 1962) is an extremely useful tool for immediate application on any tacky definitions or concepts. The elementary teacher can save hours on "how to" in arts and crafts as classroom activities by consulting the University of the State of New York's suggestions in **Art for Elementary Schools**

John J. Farrell is Director of Humanities, Briarcliff High School, Briarcliff Manor, New York.

(N.Y. State Education Dept., 1967, pb). Social studies teachers will find the suggestions for projects particularly useful. Finding sources for slide collections is often a timely chore, but one of the most valuable books for this purpose is W. H. Pierson and M. Davidson, eds., **Arts of the United States, A Pictorial Survey** (Univ. of Georgia, 1966); it pinpoints the entire history of American visual arts slide by slide, tells you where to get them, and how to go about it. Nahum Tschacbasou, ed., **Teachers' Manual for the Study of Art History and Related Courses** (American Library Color Slide, 1964, pb) is rich in illustrations and details on what slides are available in world architecture and art history, and it is cross-referenced. A physically heavy but very useful volume for finding immediate information on any of the arts is Herbert Read, **Encyclopedia of the Arts** (Meredith, 1966). For the more advanced students seeking meaning in aesthetic principles, and who do not want to be "drowned" in excessive verbiage, Clive Bell's **Art** (Capricorn, 1958) is a pleasant excursion to the "whats," "whys," and "hows"; students in the upper secondary levels are also intrigued with George Santayana's **The Sense of Beauty** (Modern Library, 1955, pb), a statement on the topic that defies time. John Dewey's **Art As Experience** (Capricorn, 1959, pb) is also a most useful motivational tool for discussion, and is readily available.

For a very helpful visual approach to the arts, pictures serve as an immediate tool for the busy teacher. For one who wants details about the most important elements of many famous paintings, see Kenneth Clark, **Looking at Pictures** (Beacon, 1968, pb). For a delightful visual treat with short textual commentaries on sculpture that provide immediate and pertinent information above the ordinary, see G. Bazin, **The History of World Sculpture** (N.Y. Graphic Society, 1968).

Theatre and architecture furnish worthwhile sources in humanities. The best anthologies for American plays are the annual publications by John Gassner, ed., **The Best American Plays** (Crown). Architecture received updated treatment in S. Giedion, **Space, Time, and Architecture** (Harvard Univ., 1966), which fills the information gap on this subject.

Films and Movies

No humanities program can ignore the place of films and filmmaking as part of the contemporary scene. For the teacher at all levels who needs all the basic details without the technical confusion, see Kirk Smallman, **Creative Film-making** (Macmillan, 1969, pb) and Paul Petzold, **All in One Movie Book** (Amphoto, 1969); the latter has the best descriptive drawings of cameras and how they work in print. Not a book, but almost essential for knowing exactly what's going on in film and where to get suitable films, the periodical *Media and Methods* is unsurpassed.

Music

The teacher who suddenly finds himself "taking on" the music section of the humanities would do well to keep Leonard Bernstein's **The Infinite Variety of Music** (Simon & Schuster, 1966) within easy reach; also see Bernstein's **The Joy of Music** (Simon & Schuster, 1963, pb), a lively treatment of the art, especially written for classroom use. Elizabeth Rogers has edited and revised M. Bauer and E. Peyser, **Music Through the Ages** (Putnam, 1967), and it has been updated for practical classroom use. When one feels dated in the musical literature, have Arthur Cohn's **Twentieth Century Music in Western Europe** (Lippincott, 1965) available for brief and vivid descriptions of major works. Nothing on the scene is as useful for understanding the recording market and how to find the best performances, and on what labels, as Howard Taubman, ed., **Guide to Listening Pleasure** (N.Y. Times, 1968); it will save days of guesswork. See also Milton Okun, ed., **Great Songs of the Sixties** (Quadrangle, 1970, pb), which includes words and music to eighty-two of the most popular songs of our time.

General Works on the Humanities

Two paperback publications on humanities-centered curriculum provide the rationale in a most coherent way. Harold Taylor, ed., **The Humanities and the Schools** (Citation, 1968, pb), a series of essays from a professional symposium, is especially eloquent on the development of affective curricula. Louise M. Berman, ed., **The Humanities and the Curriculum** (ASCD-NEA, 1967, pb) is useful for building humanities content within the traditional school subject matter, and for enlarging one's point of view of what social studies, for example, could contribute to this development. For the teacher who may have to "defend" a course in the humanities to a doubting board of education, Arthur A. Cohn, ed., **Humanistic Education and Western Civilization: Essays for Robert M. Hutchins** (Holt, 1964) presents the philosophies of some very astute authorities on the definition of a truly educated man and provides a wealth of resources for presenting a "case." Gerald Weinstein and M. Fantini, eds., **Toward Humanistic Education, A Curriculum of Affect** (Praeger, 1970) is more to the point in developing a course of study that reflects students' concerns and feelings rather than the traditional cognitive approach. Suggested teaching procedures, with a basic model for use in different environments, are especially interesting.

Thomas A. Powell, ed., **Humanities and the Social Studies** (NCSS, 1969, pb) contains useful essays on the relationships between the two subjects, and includes sections on developing curriculum in this direction. One of the most interesting programs for blending the traditional world civilization curriculum with major doses of affective materials from the humanities is detailed in *Research and Development Project to Develop, Improve, Expand and Evaluate Behavioral Goals of a Team Taught Humanities-Oriented Course in World Civilization for 9th and 10th Grade Students* (ERIC, 1970). This program would be especially helpful for those social studies and English teachers who would like to promote an interdisciplinary course that would not weaken the subject matter of either. A rather unique and provocative study of creativity, meaningful for all subjects but especially in the social studies and humanities, is H. Taylor and Gantz, **A Transactional Approach to Creativity and Its Implications for Education: Value Dilemmas in the Assessment and Development of Creative Leaders** (American Assn. for Advancement of Science, 1969, pb).

Possible alterations of learning environments to cause perceptual changes, and the motivation necessary to promote creativity are two areas worth considering when preparing a program geared to truly humanistic approaches. Of value to early childhood educators is Martin Dishart, **Arts and Humanities for Young Children** (ERIC). The visual arts, dance, literature, music and theater are the components of the tested program for grades K-3 (includes how teachers should be prepared for such creative activities). A tested program for high school seniors, with primary consideration for the values in Western civilization as its reason for being, and not tied to any traditional subject matter, may be obtained from this chapter's author.

A recent series of humanities booklets developed for use at the high school level in connection with United States history classes is entitled **Profile of America.** Developed by Richard E. Gross and Robert F. Madgic for Field Educational Publications (1971), ten booklets parallel ten periods of national history. Each contains selections from novels, short stories, biographies, poetry, dramas, etc. of or about that particular era. Songs and the art and architecture of each period are also included.

16

International Studies

JAMES M. BECKER

International studies today, like the world it seeks to understand, is in a state of ferment and change. New ideas and concepts are emerging that question many of our most cherished assumptions about international society—the notion, for example, that the only important actors in international politics are nation states; that nations are sovereign in their domestic affairs and can be influenced in only very limited ways by foreign powers; that decision-making units are not subject to internal tensions and conflicts concerning goals, policies or definitions of national interest; or that international political processes are unique and differ fundamentally from political behavior within the national unit.

This skepticism about traditional ideas, along with other social and intellectual influences, is working to propel international studies into novel and innovative directions. Historically, a major justification for the study of international relations has been the need to understand better the problems of war and peace. Added to this is the growing demand that academic studies be employed to help deal with the problems of society. All this suggests that the years ahead will see not only a continuing search for new concepts and methodologies from many different disciplines, but also a greater volume of comparative studies, renewed efforts to bridge the gap between normative and quantitative behavioral theories, and greater efforts to relate theory to practice.

This chapter can only hint at the variety of changes and debates

---

James M. Becker is Director, Social Studies Development Center, Indiana University, Bloomington, Indiana.

going on in the general field of international studies. The readings suggested here provide some indication of these developments. They also offer some of the insights and information needed in long overdue efforts to internationalize the school curriculum.

Global Perspectives

Political and economic interdependence, instantaneous worldwide communication, issues of global ecology, and rapid intercontinental travel have combined with the astronaut's image of our fragile green globe floating in space to jolt us into awareness that the threats to human survival are global in nature and that we consequently need an education about the world as a unit, not merely as a collection of separate entities or areas. A number of recent books provide such a perspective.

Barbara Ward's **Spaceship Earth** (Columbia University Press, 1966, pb) and Buckminster Fuller's **Operating Manual for Spaceship Earth** (Pocket Books, 1969) both regard our spaceship as a mess. Fuller's solution lies in the potentialities of technology. Asserting that people should not do what machines can do, Fuller recommends "general system theory" as the form of technical expertise for better piloting of spaceship earth. Barbara Ward, on the other hand, puts her faith partly in the growing awareness of our planetary crisis on the part of more "riders on the earth" and partly in increased reliance on the United Nations, trade, aid and education.

A number of other books start from premises similar to these: that we are living in a critical and precarious moment in history in which our world is, as never before, truly interdependent. Kenneth Boulding in **The Meaning of the Twentieth Century** (Harper Colophon, 1965), Richard A. Falk in **The Endangered Planet** (Random House, 1971), and C. A. W. Manning in **The Nature of International Society** (Wiley & Sons, 1962) all argue persuasively for the need for drastic changes in man's social order. Falk's concern lies primarily with world politics as related to man-in-nature; Manning stresses the "social cosmos" as a tool for thinking in a larger social context; and Boulding emphasizes the need for changing the "noosphere" (our "mind-scape" of the world) as a necessary prelude to changing our collective behavior. All three volumes offer valuable insights into the condition of man and global society.

International Relations

Man's potential for self-annihilation has transformed the field of international relations from a simple academic discipline to a study in the art and science of survival. The critical state of international affairs has also provided the impetus for many advances in this field of study, including changes in concepts and theories, new methods of research, greater use of statistical procedures for analysis and the growing availability of verifiable empirical data.

Among the new books dealing with international relations is **The Analysis of International Relations** (Prentice-Hall, 1968, pb), a brief study by Karl W. Deutsch. Asserting that men are both "incurably diverse and inescapably interdependent" and that "foreign and domestic politics are often being pushed in several contradictory directions," Deutsch goes on to warn that "the safety and prosperity of each country . . . the survival of mankind, may depend on the outcome of these multiple contests."

Three different frameworks for analyzing international affairs are presented by K. J. Holsti's **International Politics: A Framework for Analysis** (Prentice-Hall, 1967); John Burton's **Systems, States, Diplomacy and Rules** (Cambridge University Press, 1968); and John Stoessigner's **The Might of Nations: World Politics in Our Time** (Random House, 1969). Holsti emphasizes the factors that affect foreign policy-making. Burton criticizes earlier theories of relations among nations and applies systems theory to the study of international relations. And Stoessinger treats world politics in terms of two themes: the struggle for power and order (e.g., between East and West or between colonial and anti-colonial nations) and the gap between perception and reality and its effect on international affairs.

Andrew Scott's **The Functioning of the International Political System** (Macmillan, 1967, pb) provides a compact presentation of a set of assumptions, observations and propositions about international politics. His treatment of "Images, values and ideology," "Decision-making," "Conflict-escalation and abatement" and other topics provides an excellent source of insights into the changing nature of international politics. A useful handbook for comparative studies is Bruce Russett's **Trends in World Politics** (Macmillan, 1965, pb), which assesses some of the changes in the international political system. After examining such forces as communications, poverty and alignments in the United Nations, it suggests possible consequences for the future, using a variety of analytical techniques. Kenneth N. Waltz in **Man, the State, and War** (Columbia University Press, 1960, pb) presents a thoughtful analysis of the nature and causes of war and demonstrates how to analyze the causes of conflict.

International Conflict for Beginners by Roger Fisher (Harper and Row, 1969, pb) offers a refreshing, clear and, at the same time, frightening picture of the decision-making process within the State Department. The use of current problems such as Cuba, Korea, Vietnam and the Middle East in presenting ideas; the pragmatic, non-moralistic approach; and the emphasis on devising "Yesable Propositions" make this a practical, exciting handbook in the analysis of contemporary international affairs.

International Development

Television documentaries and a great variety of articles and research reports have familiarized us with the depressing statistics on illiteracy, population increase, food shortages and infant mortality. We are now aware, at least intellectually, that the gap between rich and poor nations is widening, not shrinking; and we are beginning to see that poverty can exist in even the most technologically advanced nations—like our own—side by side with affluence. The complex and varied issues involved in "development education" are beginning to receive increased attention from educators throughout the world, and this facet of international studies is now being recognized as a particularly crucial one.

Among the classics in this field are Robert L. Heilbroner's **The Great Ascent** (Harper and Row, 1963, pb) and Cyril Black's **The Dynamics of Modernization** (Harper and Row, 1967, pb). The topics treated in these two valuable books include the problems of underdevelopment, major historical patterns for studying contemporary societies and suggestions for change. **World Development: An Introductory Reader** (Macmillan, 1971), edited by Helene Castel, is a provocative, challenging book of readings that questions many of the basic assumptions about the goals and values of development as well as treating the historical, social and cultural reasons for development and underdevelopment. Distinguishing between the social, economic and political elements of development on the one hand, and the ultimate goal of human development on the other, the book seeks to place the development process in a context of human dignity and justice. C. Welch (ed.) in **Political Modernization: A Reader in Comparative Political Change** (Wadsworth, 1967, pb) seeks to clarify several approaches to the comparative study of modernization while tracing patterns of world change and their political implications. And Lester Pearson's **Crisis in Development** (Praeger, 1970) and Gunnar Myrdal's **The Challenge of World Poverty** (Pantheon, 1970) are comprehensive "state of world" reports with calls to action as well as valuable information on this issue.

Foreign Policy

Skeptics have long argued that the intricacies of foreign policy should be left to the experts, and debates such as those surrounding Vietnam and the anti-ballistic missile system have raised this issue again. Such abdication is unacceptable to most people of democratic temperament. In fact, there is substantial evidence that policy-makers and laymen alike are fallible in gathering and interpreting data. Becoming well informed about foreign policy is clearly not easy, but rather than abandoning the task altogether we should recognize our limitations and seek ways to compensate for them.

Fortunately, there are some very useful books to help with this task. John Lovell's **Foreign Policy in Perspective** (Holt, Rinehart and Winston, 1970) is an excellent introduction to many of the complexities of the foreign policy process in the United States and provides a helpful guide to the reader who wants to make his own independent assessment of foreign policy. Burton M. Sapin's **The Making of U.S. Foreign Policy** (Praeger, 1967, pb; Brookings Institution Study, available in cloth edition from Brookings Institution), and Henry Kissinger's **American Foreign Policy: Three Essays** (Norton, 1969, pb) focus on the formulation and administration of foreign policy within the country. And the military aspect of foreign policy can be approached through several useful and non-technical books including Raymond Aron's **The Great Debate: Theories of Nuclear Strategy** (Doubleday, 1965); Thomas C. Shelling's **Arms and Influence** (Yale University Press, 1966); and Bruce Russett's **What Price Vigilance?** (Yale University Press, 1970, pb).

International Organizations

Recent years have seen a rapid growth of organizations with links across national boundaries. Many of the new global organizations (or proposals for reorganization of old ones) involve UN agencies or regional groupings. In addition, however, there has also been a startling rise in the number of other kinds of international organizations, non-governmental as well as governmental. None has developed as rapidly or created as much concern as the multinational corporation. The increasingly complex and decentralized network of multinational corporations and other international organizations has engendered both hope and fear: hope that the existence of numerous and varied organizations with overlapping memberships may help control violence; fear that proliferation of organizations, with all the competitive wastefulness this entails, may reduce efficiency while intensifying tensions and conflicts.

Raymond Vernon's **Sovereignty at Bay** (Basic Books, 1971); Sidney E. Rolfe's **The Multinational Corporation in the World Economy** (Praeger, 1970); and Jean-Jacques Servan-Schreiber's **The American Challenge** (Avon, 1968) all deal with the impact of radical and unprecedented technology — especially in American industry, education and information processing — on international events and politico-economic conditions. Servan-Schreiber urges Europe to rise to the "American challenge" or risk being condemned to a permanent state of inferiority. Jack C. Plano and Robert E. Riggs in **Forging World Order** (Macmillan, 1967) present a multifaceted study of the development of regional and global organizations. They approach the field from the premise that "politics is all cut from the same cloth at all levels of human activity," an assumption that enables them to draw some interesting parallels between politics in diverse realms of human endeavor.

The growth of international organizations, especially as this relates to the future of the United Nations, is among the concerns of Inis L. Claude in **The Changing United Nations** (Random House, 1967, pb); Ernest B. Haas in **The Tangle of Hopes** (Prentice-Hall, 1969); and Leon E. Gordeneker, ed., in **The United Nations in International Politics** (Princeton University Press, 1971). Haas presents a strong case for greater centralization at the national, regional and global levels. In particular, he urges creation of non-governmental planning boards and development of greater collaboration among the developing countries in fashioning a common approach to their trade-aid-money needs. The Gordeneker volume presents the answers of a number of experts to such questions as: How can we understand the actions of the United Nations? How can we assess the prospects for the future of the UN?

World Law and World Order

Although widespread support exists in this country for strengthening international law, the extent to which international law should or actually does determine or modify the policies of government is still the subject of much debate. Because of a renewed interest in peace education, however, the study of world law, as one means of working toward a more peaceful world, is attracting increased attention and interest.

Perhaps the "bible" in the world law field is **World Peace Through World Law** by Grenville Clark and Louis Sohn (Harvard University Press, 1971, pb). Another work, **Toward a Theory of War Prevention** by Richard A. Falk and Saul H. Mendlovitz (World Law Fund, 1966, pb), presents papers by government officials, journalists and social scientists on the possibilities of evolving an effective war-prevention system. Many of the ideas found in the Clark-Sohn volume are also dealt with in this book.

Louis Henkin in **How Nations Behave: Law and Foreign Policy** (Columbia University Press, 1968, pb) and Arthur Larson, *et al.* in **Sovereignty Within the Law** (Rand McNally, 1965) examine the role of international law in influencing the behavior of sovereign states. Condemning unilateralism in an interdependent world, both offer a clear presentation of the benefits of international law. David Mitrany's **A Working Peace System** (Quadrangle Books, 1966) and Michael Barkun's **Law Without Sanctions** (Yale University Press, 1968) emphasize the relationship between law and society and stress the need for voluntary cooperation and the importance of law as a means for maintaining change within acceptable limits.

While the books mentioned here constitute but a small fraction of recent works, they indicate something of the range and diversity that characterize international studies today and suggest a number of approaches or thrusts which might serve as a basis for organizing units or courses in international studies.

17

Law and Justice

ROBERT H. RATCLIFFE

The need for law-related content in social studies education has long been a truism in American education. Developmental work conducted over the past half-dozen years has resulted in the broad-based education of teachers in both the substantive and methodological spheres of law-focused social studies education. A basic premise of educators engaged in the field has been that classroom teachers in the social studies have had less than adequate preparation for teaching students about the law. Similarly, there has been a dearth of information about materials that can satisfy the needs of teachers and others interested in the development of law-focused elementary and secondary curricula. This chapter contains references to books that range from the historical development of our legal system to contemporary urban legal problems and basic reference tools.

Legal Development and Reasoning

A number of succinct statements regarding the development of the law and the legal reasoning process are available to the teacher in a group of three books. Frederick G. Kempin, Jr., **Legal History: Law and Social Change** excellently analyzes the development of the courts, the jury system, and the lawyer as they grew and emerged from the era of the Common Law; William Zelermyer, **Process of Legal Reasoning** ex-

Robert H. Ratcliffe is Executive Director of the Law in American Society Foundation and Associate Professor of Education at the University of Illinois at Chicago Circle, Chicago, Illinois.

plores in detail legal reasoning from trial through final appeal; and Lew Mayers, **Machinery of Justice** (all three Prentice-Hall, 1963, pb) specifies the development of rules and general civil, criminal, and military legal procedures. An in-depth, professional treatment of this area, provided by Harry W. Jones, **Materials for Legal Method** (Foundation, 1970), can be recommended for the development of skills in case analysis and legal principles plus use of law library reference works.

Law in Prose, Including Urban Specialties

Voluminous literature has grown up around the law. For the purposes of the teacher, René A. Wormser, **The Story of the Law** (Simon & Schuster, 1962, pb) presents an informed overview of the law throughout history. Anthony Lewis, **Gideon's Trumpet** (Random House, 1964, pb), a modern classic, describes a pauper's persistent effort to assert his right to counsel, an excellent description of Supreme Court functions. In Gordon E. Baker, **Reapportionment Revolution** (Random House, 1966, pb), comprehensive surveys report legislative apportionment in the United States. Neil Sheehan, Smith, Kenworthy, and Butterfield, **Pentagon Papers** (Bantam, 1971, pb) provides a recent example of an important principle in the area of constitutional law. A decision in this case demonstrates that at least five justices must agree via the same pattern of reasoning for a rule to extend beyond the case at bar. Here the six-man majority follows six separate patterns of reasoning. Finally Maximilian Kössler, **Masterpieces of Legal Fiction** (Lawyers Co-op, 1964) is a charming, witty exposition to enrich the reader's understanding of the legal process.

An interesting perspective in the area of urban legal problems may be obtained from Paul Freund, **On Law and Justice** (Harvard Univ., 1968). Teachers interested in a comprehensive bibliography in the area of urban living will profit from Carol Katz, **The Law and the Low Income Consumer** (New York Univ., 1968, pb), which represents the basic publishing efforts of the national clearing house in the field of social welfare law. William C. Kvaraceus, **Dynamics of Delinquency** (Merrill, 1967) presents teachers with an important statement regarding the phenomenon of delinquency.

Most legal reference materials specialize in a single area of the law. One of the most valuable *general* reference tools available to the teacher is Henry C. Black, **Black's Law Dictionary** (West, 1968). The best single volume for classroom use in the area of Constitutional Law is **Constitution of the United States: Analysis and Interpretation** (USGPO, 1964), which contains a wealth of analytical and interpretive material on Constitutional Law cases decided through the middle of 1964. For a well-edited selection in the area of human rights, see Zechariah Chafee, Jr., **Documents on Fundamental Human Rights** (Atheneum, 1963, pb), which contains documents dating from 1330-1951. An interpretation of one of the more controversial laws of modern times is the excellent Department of Justice, **Handbook on the Law of Search and Seizure** (USGPO, 1968). A practical description of the legal rights of citizens under the age of twenty-one is contained in Jean Strouse, **Up Against the Law** (New American Library, 1970, pb).

Resource Materials, Including Legal Cases and Teacher's Guides

There are many excellent books that can profitably be used as prime resources for developing effective curricula. One of the best is Isidore Starr, **The Supreme Court and Contemporary Issues** (Encyclopedia Britannica, 1969, pb), a lucid, topical treatment of six areas of constitutional interest. Paul C. Bartholomew, **Leading Cases on the Constitution** (Littlefield, 1970, pb) is a highly useful book containing summaries of the major decisions of the United States Supreme Court from the time of its establishment. Milton R. Konvitz, ed., **Bill of Rights Reader: Leading Constitutional Cases** (Cornell, 1968) is widely regarded as indispensable to a current understanding of the rights, powers, and obligations of individuals as well as authorities. For a comprehensive selection of significant Supreme Court decisions, Lockhart, Kamisar and Choper, **Constitutional Law: Cases — Comments — Questions** (West, 1970) is highly recommended. Readers interested in a unique perspective on due process are referred to William M. Kunstler, **And Justice for All** (Oceana, 1963), which contains ten cases ranging from Mrs. Surratt to Engel V. Vitale.

In the area of method, a number of useful volumes in paperback form are available to the teacher. Sections of books are recommended in other chapters. (Massialas and Zevin; Norris M. Sanders; Raths, Harmin, Simon; Bruner; and Allen, Fleckensten, Lyon include methods and/or materials for teachers of law and justice.) For practical bibliographies of books and audio-visual materials see a series of six, Robert H. Ratcliffe, ed., **Justice in Urban America: Teacher's Guide,** and a series of three, Robert H. Ratcliffe, ed., **Trailmarks of Liberty: Teacher's Guides** (Houghton Mifflin, 1970, 1971, pb).

18

Mass Communication in Society

ERNEST C. HYNDS

Everyone who hopes to function effectively in today's increasingly complex world must have some understanding and knowledge of the mass media and how to use them. The media provide information about government, business, education, social affairs, sports, the weather, and myriad other subjects. They influence both collective and individual decisions. They provide entertainment for millions. Through their advertising they help turn the wheels of the free enterprise system. By providing a forum for information and a constant check on government, they help keep the democratic system in operation. This chapter will suggest some recent books that can provide insight into the roles of the media and their relationships to society.

The Big Picture

Several books published recently can help the teacher obtain a good overview of the mass media. The most comprehensive single volume is Edwin Emery, Phillip H. Ault, and Warren K. Agee, **Introduction to Mass Communications** (Dodd, Mead, 1970). It gives a balanced presentation of all the media and includes a 35-page annotated bibliography. The functions and significance of newspapers, radio, television, and general magazines are discussed effectively in Verne E. Edwards, Jr., **Journalism in a Free Society** (Brown, 1970). Edwards seeks to inspire belief in the

---

Ernest C. Hynds is Associate Professor of Journalism, School of Journalism, University of Georgia, Athens, Georgia.

real meaning of press freedom and a more intelligent evaluation of press performance. A well-organized view of the media in their cultural setting is provided by William L. Rivers, Theodore Peterson, and Jay W. Jensen, **Mass Media and Modern Society** (Holt, 1971); a good discussion of communication ethics is offered in Rivers and Wilbur Schramm, **Responsibility in Mass Communication** (Harper & Row, 1969); and a sampling of media professionals' views on responsibility is included in Gerald Gross, ed., **The Responsibility of the Press** (Fleet, 1966, pb). Media problems and prospects are analyzed by John Hohenberg in **The News Media: A Journalist Looks at His Profession** (Holt, 1968), and the possible future content, form, and methods of distributing information media are explored by Ben H. Bagdikian in **Information Machines: Their Impact on Men and the Media** (Harper & Row, 1971).

Media History

The best single volume on the history of American journalism is provided by Edwin Emery, **The Press and America: An Interpretative History of Journalism** (Prentice-Hall, 1972). It is particularly effective in correlating developments in journalism with political, economic, and social trends. A good study of individual journalists and individual publications, particularly newspapers, is offered in Frank Luther Mott, **American Journalism: A History: 1690-1960** (Macmillan, 1962). Magazine history is explored more fully in James Playsted Wood, **Magazines in the United States** (Ronald, 1970), Theodore Peterson, **Magazines in the Twentieth Century** (Univ. of Illinois, 1964), and John Tebbel, **The American Magazine: A Compact History** (Hawthorn, 1969). Tebbel also has done **The Compact History of the American Newspaper** (Hawthorn, 1969). Broadcasting history is explored in three volumes by Eric Barnouw. They are **A Tower of Babel** (to 1933), **The Golden Web** (1933-1953), and **The Image Empire: A History of Broadcasting in the United States from 1953** (Oxford Univ., 1966, 1968, 1970). Additional information about the black press is provided both in Martin Dann, ed., **The Black Press (1827-1890)** (Putnam, 1971) and Roland E. Wolseley, **The Black Press, U.S.A.** (Iowa State Univ., 1971).

Newspapers, Magazines, Books

Most of the recent books dealing specifically with newspapers concentrate on reporting and other techniques, which are not the primary concern of this chapter. One of the most useful general books is John C. Merrill, **The Elite Press: Great Newspapers of the World** (Pitman, 1968, pb). Merrill presents profiles of 40 "great" newspapers, including a number from the United States, and explains why they are considered great. Problems and values of newspapers are discussed by John Tebbel in his **Open Letter to Newspaper Readers** (Heineman, 1968, pb), and the history, functions, and audiences of the alternative or underground press are described by Robert J. Glessing in **The Underground Press in America** (Indiana Univ., 1970). Some readers may find some of the language and illustrations cited offensive, but this is the best account so far of the underground press movement.

A good general account of the magazine industry is provided in Roland E. Wolseley, **Understanding Magazines** (Iowa State Univ., 1969), and the extent and operation of specialized magazines is explored by James L. C. Ford, **Magazines for Millions** (Southern Illinois Univ., 1970). A good survey of the book publishing field is Charles G. Madison's **Book Publishing in America** (McGraw-Hill, 1967).

Advertising, Public Relations

Two of the best advertising studies are S. Watson Dunn, **Advertising: Its Role in Modern Marketing** (Holt, 1969) and Charles H. Sandage and Vernon Fryburger, **Advertising Theory and Practice** (Irwin, 1971). Both do a good job of relating advertising to social and economic affairs generally.

The best overall picture of public relations is provided by Scott M. Cutlip and Allen M. Center, **Effective Public Relations** (Prentice-Hall, 1971). It deals effectively with history, theory, and contemporary practices. Other useful works are Bertrand R. Canfield, **Public Relations: Principles, Cases and Problems** (Irwin, 1968) and Philip Lesley, ed., **Public Relations Handbook** (Prentice-Hall, 1968).

Radio, Television, Film

The best overview of broadcasting in the United States is offered by Sydney W. Head, **Broadcasting in America: A Survey of Television and Radio** (Houghton Mifflin, 1972). It deals with all aspects of those media, makes an assessment of influence, and includes a helpful bibliography. A world overview of broadcasting is provided by Walter B. Emery, **National and International Systems of Broadcasting: Their History, Operation and Control** (Michigan State Univ., 1969). Radio, television, and film all are discussed by various authorities in David Manning White and Richard Averson, eds., **Sight, Sound and Society** (Beacon, 1968). The great potential of cable television is explored in Herman W. Land Associates, **Television and the Wired City: A Study of the Implications of a Change in the Mode of Transmission** (Natl. Assn. of Broadcasters, 1968). The educational potential of radio and television is discussed in Herman W. Land Associates, **The Hidden Medium: A Status Report on Educational Radio in the United States** (Natl. Assn. of Broadcasters, 1967) and Allen E. Koenig and Duane B. Hill, **The Farther Vision: Educational Television Today** (Univ. of Wisconsin, 1967, pb). The status of motion pictures is discussed in R. S. Randall, **Censorship of the Movies: The Social and Political Control of a Mass Medium** (Univ. of Wisconsin, 1967, pb).

Further Possibilities

Those who wish a more extensive bibliography on the mass media should refer to Warren C. Price, **The Literature of Journalism: An Annotated Bibliography** (Univ. of Minnesota, 1959); Price and Calder M. Pickett, comps., **An Annotated Journalism Bibliography 1958-1968** (Univ. of Minnesota, 1970); and the periodic listings in such publications as *Journalism Quarterly*. Slides, filmstrips, films, kinescopes, audio tapes and discs and television tapes also are available to help students learn about the mass media. A number are listed in Gary Coll and W. Manion Rice, **Selected Bibliography of Audio-Visual Aids for Journalism** (Southern Illinois Univ., 1968). Finally, the media themselves provide a continuing source of study as they expand their coverage and influence and become even more vital to contemporary human life.

19

Philosophy and Social Values

JOHN R. PALMER

There is no single introduction to philosophy which provides a comprehensive survey of the questions encompassed by the field. One can philosophize about any human activity and each is at least potentially of concern to social educators. It is useful, however, to select some of the areas within philosophy that are of obvious import to social education.

General Philosophy of Education

Many books of readings and original works presenting a comprehensive philosophy of education are available but the quality is very uneven. **Modern Movements in Educational Philosophy** edited by Van Cleve Morris (Houghton Mifflin, 1969, pb), and **The Concept of Education** edited by R. S. Peters (Humanities, 1967) are provocative collections of writings dealing with philosophical questions central to the process of education. Useful works by a single author, which demonstrate the development of a unified philosophy of education, include H. S. Broudy, **Building a Philosophy of Education** (Prentice-Hall, 1961) and Philip Smith, **Philosophy of Education** (Harper & Row, 1965). The work of John Dewey is obviously central to American philosophy of education. His 1916 **Democracy and Education** (Free Press, 1971, pb) and his 1910 original, **How We Think** (Heath, 1971, pb) are two of his

John R. Palmer is Professor of History and Curriculum and Instruction, School of Education, University of Wisconsin, Madison, Wisconsin.

many works that give direction to social education. The influence of Dewey's thought is evident in such works as **Reflective Thinking: The Method of Education** by Gordon Hullfish and Philip Smith (Dodd, 1961) and **Teaching High School Social Studies** by Maurice Hunt and Lawrence Metcalf (Harper and Row, 1968). There is now available in one volume a comprehensive bibliography of books, monographs, and articles in philosophy of education organized by topics. **Philosophy of Education, An Organization of Topics and Selected Sources** by H. S. Broudy and others (Univ. of Illinois, 1967, pb) is an invaluable aid as each of hundreds of sources is briefly summarized as well as listed by topic.

Values: In Society and in the Classroom

It is difficult to engage in an analysis of values without referring to contents of the classic works of Plato, Aristotle, Epicurus, Hobbes and so forth. These philosophers developed many of the positions and problems that still are the focus of controversy. A selection of their writings found in A. I. Melden, **Ethical Theories** (Prentice-Hall, 1955) provides an introduction to the standard problems of value theory. Contemporary theories of particular interest to social educators are presented in Kurt Baier, **The Moral Point of View: A Rational Basis of Ethics** (Random House, 1965, pb); Abraham Edel, **Ethical Judgment: The Use of Science in Ethics** (Free Press, 1955, pb); Joseph Fletcher, **Situation Ethics: The New Morality** (Westminster, 1966, pb); and Paul Kurtz, **Moral Problems in Contemporary Society** (Prentice-Hall, 1969, pb). While it must be granted that none of these volumes can be understood quickly and easily, they represent the intellectual problems that are central to the process of valuing.

Typically a matter of sociological investigation, the American value system is apparently moving to a complex of sub-systems and developing increasing diversity. Useful studies of contemporary American values include Jules Henry, **Culture Against Man** (Vintage, 1965, pb); Gunnar Myrdal, **An American Dilemma** (Harper & Row, 1944, pb); Robin Williams, Jr., **American Society** (Knopf, 1970); and Herbert Muller, **The Children of Frankenstein** (Indiana, 1970). The peculiar value context of education and the student's role in it has been dealt with in the volume by Jules Henry cited above as well as in Edgar Friedenberg, **Coming of Age in America** (Vintage, 1965, pb) and Robert Dreeben in **On What is Learned in School** (Addison, 1968).

Introduction to Moral Education by John Wilson and others (Penguin, 1967, pb) provides a comprehensive theoretical analysis of the place of values in formal schooling. The two most significant empirical approaches to value development are summarized in the lecture by Lawrence Kohlberg included in **Moral Education: Five Lectures,** edited by Theodore and Nancy Sizer (Harvard Univ., 1970) and Milton Rokeach's **Beliefs, Attitudes, and Values** (Jossey-Bass, 1969). Fred Newmann, Louis Raths, and Lawrence Metcalf provide quite different detailed instructional strategies for dealing with value questions.

Social Philosophy

The conflict between the building of social consensus and the promotion of a more open society leads ultimately to different interpretations of the good society and the role of institutions as agents of social control. John Dewey's non-political definition of democracy still provides a touchstone for a consideration of democratic social philosophy apart from the typical approach of political science. The contemporary literature that bears on the issues students and teachers might consider is extremely large and represents the research and thinking of virtually every discipline. **Contemporary Political Theory** by Eugene Meehan (Dorsey, 1967) is a very readable critical survey of contemporary political theory as it has been developed within the discipline of political science. **Power and Community** edited by Philip Green and Sanford Levinson (Vintage, 1970, pb) raises questions about academic political theory and suggests alternatives. A number of efforts have been made to contrast the theory of American democracy and its practice. Edmond Cahn, **The Predicament of Democratic Man** (Macmillan, 1961, pb); G. William Domhoff, **Who Rules America?** (Prentice-Hall, 1967, pb); and Bertram Gross, ed., **A Great Society?** (Basic, 1966) offer several perspectives on the condition of American Democracy. Social philosophy is being influenced by the renewed interest in the biological nature of man as presented in Robert Ardrey, **The Social Contract** (Atheneum, 1970) and Konrad Lorenz, **On Aggression** (Harcourt, 1966, pb).

While the development of the concept of black power in America has many foci, the political theory essential to it is suggested by Stokely Carmichael and Charles Hamilton in **Black Power** (Vintage, 1967, pb) and its world context by Frantz Fanon in **The Wretched of the Earth** (Grove, 1963, pb). The social philosophies implicit in many blueprints of the future have raised doubts about the continuation of democratic institutions and the "liberal" assumption of social equilibrium. B. F. Skinner's **Walden Two** (Macmillan, 1962, pb) and George Orwell's **Nineteen Eighty-Four** (New American Library, 1949, pb) are two classics that many students could read and enjoy. Possible implications of developments in technology are portrayed by Robert Boguslow in **The New Utopians** (Prentice-Hall, 1969, pb). Peter Berger and Thomas Luckmann's **The Social Construction of Reality** (Anchor Doubleday, 1967, pb) suggests that formal education may have little influence on the social philosophy of students. It also implies that social experience may be more crucial than a rationally developed theory in determining what actually occurs in any society. In any case, it is very possible that we are in the midst of developing new social philosophies. The problem for the teacher, then, is not one of presenting a carefully formulated social philosophy but rather one of putting students in touch with the diverse elements that might be considered in developing a social philosophy. While social philosophy is rarely taught as a subject, it has a major place in both the formal and hidden curricula of all schools. Many unit books in the AEP Public Issues Series prepared by Donald Oliver and Fred Newmann and the readings presented in **From Left to Right** edited by Herbert Robb and Raymond Sobel (Benziger, 1968, pb) are designed so that a consideration of social philosophy will likely occur.

Philosophy of History and Social Science

Recent emphasis on structure and process in social studies education requires a considerable knowledge of the nature of the several disciplines. **The Nature of Social Science** by George Homans (Harcourt, 1967, pb) provides a simple introduction to the philosophy of social science. More difficult but essential to a thorough analysis of the nature of social science are Ernest Nagel, **The Structure of Science** (Harcourt, 1961) and Peter Winch, **The Idea of a Social Science** (Humanities, 1958). The growing skepticism about the validity of social science methodology is voiced by W. G. Runciman in **Sociology in Its Place and Other Essays** (Cambridge Univ., 1970). The philosophy of history comes in many forms. The most useful volume for teachers is **Studies in the Nature and Teaching of History** edited by W. H. Burston and D. Thompson (Humanities, 1967). An excellent introduction to both the speculative and critical philosophies of history is **Ideas of History** edited by Ronald Nash (Dutton, 1969, pb). The impact of the consideration of the nature of disciplines on curriculum and teaching method is represented by much of the output of the social studies curriculum projects of the 1960's. Some brief theoretical papers are provided along with typical curricular outcomes by Martin Feldman and Eli Seifman. The nature of social science inquiry is set forth in Ronald Lippitt, **The Teacher's Role in Social Science Investigation** (Science Research Associates, 1969, pb).

20

Population and Urbanism

ARTHUR E. SODERLIND

The study of population and urbanism can be an important link between the natural and the social sciences. The recent rapid increase in the human population of the world as the result of more and better health services has created problems and challenges throughout the world. The migration of peoples from one area to another has reached proportions never before realized. In the United States more people now live in cities and the surrounding areas than at any other time in history.

Population

A best seller in paperback, Paul R. Ehrlich, **Population Bomb,** (Ballantine, 1968, pb) has helped arouse the world to the seriousness of overpopulation. The author's premise is that "if the human race goes on reproducing at its present rate, it will breed itself out of existence." A more scholarly treatment by the same author and his wife, Anna H. Ehrlich, is **Population, Resources, Environment: Issues in Human Ecology** (Freeman, 1970). Other viewpoints are expressed in Ronald Freedman, ed., **Population: The Vital Revolution** (Doubleday, 1964, pb), Charles B. Nam, ed., **Population and Society** (Houghton Mifflin, 1968), and the second edition of William Petersen, **Population** (Macmillan, 1969). A somewhat older book which is good for a quick informative overview is Philip M. Hauser, **Population Perspectives** (Rutgers Univ.,

---

Arthur E. Soderlind is Social Studies Consultant, Bureau of Elementary and Secondary Education, State Department of Education, Hartford, Connecticut.

1962). Dean Fraser, **People Problem: What You Should Know about Growing Population and Vanishing Resources** (Indiana Univ., 1971) and Joseph D. Tydings, **Born to Starve** (Morrow, 1971, pb) relate the population explosion and overpopulation in human terms and social awareness. Lincoln H. Day and Alice Taylor Day's **Too Many Americans** (Dell, 1968) focuses the attention on the United States.

The relationships of the food resources of the world and population are dealt with in George Borgström, **Hungry Planet: The Modern World at the Edge of Famine** (Macmillan, 1965, pb) and in William Paddock and Paul Paddock, **Famine 1975!** (Little, Brown, 1967, pb). Colin Clark, **Population Growth and Land Use** (St. Martin's, 1968), Preston Cloud, ed., **Resources and Man** (Freeman, 1969), and Donald Bogue, **Principles of Demography** (Wiley, 1969) also consider the topic. C. P. Idyll's **The Sea Against Hunger** (Crowell, 1970) discusses the potential of the sea as an important food supplier while the "green revolution" and the development of new high-yield grains are discussed in Lester R. Brown, **Seeds of Change** (Praeger, 1970, pb).

Family planning around the world is analyzed within the context of national as well as cultural, religious, social and economic considerations in Stanley Johnson, **Life Without Birth** (Little, Brown, 1971) and in S. J. Behrman, ed., **Fertility and Family Planning: A World View** (Michigan, 1969, pb). A French writer with no particular axe to grind is Alfred Sauvy, **Fertility and Survival: Population Problems from Malthus to Mao Tse-tung** (Criterion, 1962).

Several volumes written for advanced young people can give the reader a good overview. They are Fairfield Osborn, ed., **Our Crowded Planet: Essays on the Pressures of Population** (Doubleday, 1962), Tadd Fisher, **Our Overcrowded World** (Parents Magazine, 1970), and Melvin A. Benarde, **Race Against Famine** (Macrae Smith, 1970). For more advanced students two books of readings are Louise B. Young, ed., **Population in Perspective** (Oxford Univ., 1968) and the second edition of American Assembly, **The Population Dilemma** (Prentice-Hall, 1970).

Urbanism

Classic treatments of the city in historical perspective are Lewis Mumford, **The City in History** (Harcourt, 1961) and Wolf Schneider, **Babylon Is Everywhere** (McGraw-Hill, 1963). Gideon Sjoberg, **The Preindustrial City: Past and Present** (Free Press, 1969, pb) is a survey of the very early ancient civilized society. Jane Jacob's **Death and Life of Great American Cities** (Random House, 1961, pb) upset most of the traditional notions of how cities grow and what makes them live and die. The two-volume series by Blake McKelvey, **Urbanization of America: 1860-1915,** and **Emergence of Metropolitan America: 1915-1966** (Rutgers Univ., 1962, 1968) give a panoramic study of urban society over the past hundred years. Serious students of American history should also study Charles N. Glaab and A. T. Brown, **A History of Urban America** (Macmillan, 1967, pb). Intellectual reactions to the American city are collected in Morton White, **Intellectual Versus the City: From Thomas Jefferson to Frank Lloyd Wright** (Harvard Univ., 1962, pb). A brief history of American cities written for young people is S. Carl Hirsch, **Cities Are People** (Viking, 1968).

A survey of contemporary urban problems is covered in Charles Abrams, **City Is the Frontier** (Harper & Row, 1964, pb), and fifteen social scientists examine urbanization from five academic disciplines in Philip M. Hauser, ed., **Study of Urbanization** (Wiley, 1966). The September 1965 issue of *Scientific American* has been published as Dennis Flanagan, ed., **Cities** (Knopf, 1965). The diversity and complexity of the urban problems are reflected in James Q. Wilson, ed., **Metropolitan Enigma: Inquiries Into the Nature and Dimensions of America's Urban Crisis** (Harvard Univ., 1968, pb). A study of urban and regional development planning as a means of moderating the growth of metropolitan areas is made in Lloyd Rodwin, **Nations and Cities: A Comparison of Strategies for Urban Growth** (Houghton Mifflin, 1970). J. Brian McLoughlin, **Urban and Regional Planning: A Systems Approach** (Praeger, 1970) is excellent for land-use planning.

A series of case studies of federal-city urban relationships is published in Roscoe C. Martin, **Cities and the Federal System** (Atherton, 1965). In Robert C. Weaver, **Dilemmas of Urban America** (Harvard Univ., 1965, pb) the head of the U.S. Housing and Home Finance Agency admits the system's failings and points out how they can be overcome. Coverage of metropolitan government and of political processes and the urban power structure forms the basis of John C. Bollens, **Metropolis: Its People, Politics, and Economic life** (Harper & Row, 1965). There is intensive consideration of community power and political decisions in relation to schooling in **Politics of Urban Education** (Praeger, 1969, pb) by Marilyn M. Gittell and A. G. Hevesi.

Jean Gottmann, **Megalopolis: The Urbanized Northeastern Seaboard of the United States** (Twentieth Century Fund, 1961, pb) analyzes the dynamics of urbanization to show the interdependence of areas. These ideas have been somewhat simplified in Wolf Von Eckhardt, **Challenge of Megalopolis** (Macmillan, 1964, pb) and in Jean Gottmann, ed., **Metropolis on the Move: Geographers Look at Urban Sprawl** (Wiley, 1966, pb).

The concern for the aesthetics of cities is covered in Lawrence Halprin, **Cities** (Reinhold, 1963). Peter Blake, **God's Own Junkyard: Planned Deteriorations of America's Landscape** (Holt, 1963, pb) is a pictorial essay contrasting the ugliness of the United States with its beauty. Other aspects of the city are dealt with in Victor Gruen, **Heart of Our Cities: Urban Crisis, Diagnosis and Cure** (Simon & Schuster, 1964, pb), Harold

Lewis Malt, **Furnishing the City** (McGraw-Hill, 1970), and Neil W. Chamberlain, ed., **Business and the Cities: A Book of Relevant Readings** (Basic Books, 1971).

Also a prime local example is a book which differs from those already discussed that should be read and studied if only because it presents a geographic analysis of a single city through a magnificent collection of photographs, maps, and text. This collection is entitled **Chicago: Growth of a Metropolis** and was compiled by Harold M. Mayer and Richard C. Wade (Univ. of Chicago, 1969). It portrays almost every physical aspect of urban growth of Chicago over a period of 140 years, and suggests what a social studies teacher might do in helping students examine their own city and its environs.

A case study of a metropolis school system is set forth by Peter Schrag in **Village School Downtown: Politics and Education: Boston Report** (Beacon, 1967, pb). Suggested instructional methods by open inquiry in contrast to an expository-deductive approach are described by Richard Wisniewski in **New Teachers in Urban Schools: An Inside View** (Random House, 1967, pb), and Abraham Bernstein, **Education of Urban Population** (Random House, 1967, pb). Inner-city schools with low socioeconomic status compare unfavorably with schools of high socioeconomic status as found in the analysis of data from the National Principalship Study, edited by Robert E. Herriott and N. H. St. John, **Social Class and the Urban School: The Impact of Pupil Background on Teachers and Pupils** (Wiley, 1966). Anselm L. Strauss, ed., **American City: A Sourcebook of Urban Imagery** (Aldine, 1968) shows that there is a lack of historical perspective on the rhetoric of public issues. And instructional ideas for teachers appear in P. G. Kontos and J. J. Murphy, eds., **Teaching Urban Youth: A Sourcebook for Urban Education** (Wiley, 1967, pb).

21

Social Problems, Social Planning, and Change

WILLIAM M. HERING, JR.

One definition of a social problem is based on consensus; if members of a society consider an existing condition to be at odds with established norms (the way things ought to be) it is a social problem. A second definition is that social problems are conditions which, by reason of their existence, may have harmful consequences for society even if there is no widespread concern over the condition. Both perspectives are considered in this chapter. And both lead to a common conclusion that societies have problems, and that solutions ought to be proposed and implemented.

This chapter cites a few outstanding general works on social problems, books dealing with social planning, the ways and means for dealing with social problems, and some works which examine social systems undergoing change as a consequence of attempts to deal with social problems. The intent of this chapter is to present these topics within a problems perspective—a perspective frequently employed in social studies classrooms.

General Social Problems

Some of the best general books on social problems are edited anthologies. Single-authored texts which include many topics frequently suffer from lack of expertise in certain areas, resulting in an

---

William M. Hering, Jr., is in the Department of Secondary and Continuing Education, College of Education, University of Illinois, Urbana, Illinois.

uneven bookwide treatment. Of the edited anthologies, Howard Becker's **Social Problems: A Modern Approach** (Wiley, 1967) is one of the more difficult but intellectually rewarding. The most complete reader is **Social Problems: Persistent Challenges** (Holt, 1969, pb), edited by Edward McDonagh and Jon Simpson. Although both include selections by acknowledged experts on each topic, McDonagh and Simpson include more topics with shorter selections; Becker has fewer topics, greater depth, and selections written specifically for this volume. A very different anthology, **America's Troubles: A Casebook on Social Conflict** (Prentice-Hall, 1969, pb) edited by Howard Freeman and Norman Kurtz, departs from the usual pattern and includes 28 of 40 readings from popular newspapers and magazines. Most of these describe accounts of conflict processes associated with social problems. Teachers will find the Becker volume useful if they have little preparation in the area, the McDonagh volume an excellent source of short articles for reference, and the Freeman collection of readings helpful in providing specific examples of the theoretical orientation of the other two works.

Social problems are present in all societies, although there are few books which provide adequate transnational coverage. Two which provide complementary perspectives are **Comparative Perspectives on Social Problems,** Vytautas Kavolis, ed. (Little, Brown, 1971, pb) and **Comparative Social Problems,** S. N. Eisenstadt, ed. (Free Press, 1964). Although the Kavolis book is more recent, readers should include the Eisenstadt volume as a more precise and analytical treatment.

Social Planning

Social planning is an attempt to deal with the exigencies of any society faced with social problems. The easiest introduction to the subject is Raymond Mack's **Transforming America** (Random House, 1967, pb). It can be profitably read in conjunction with **Radical Perspectives on Social Problems,** Frank Lindenfeld, ed. (Macmillan, 1968, pb). Mack considers six policy questions and relates each to current sociological knowledge. Lindenfeld presents articles representative of radical solutions to similar questions; taken together, the reader can appreciate the importance of differing perspectives on these topics. Another approach to social planning is found in future analysis, the forecasting of trends with suggested alternatives. A useful volume is **The Year 2000** (Macmillan, 1967) by Herman Kahn and Anthony Wiener, which uses straight line projections and scenarios to illustrate planning alternatives. These alternatives are more carefully documented than those in **Agenda for the Nation,** Kermit Gordon, ed. (Brookings Institution, 1968, pb), but the latter is more useful for general reading. The Kahn and Wiener book is an important reference, and provides extensive graphic and tabular information. Social planning focused exclusively on domestic questions such as welfare, family planning and urbanism is analyzed in Alvin Schorr's **Explorations in Social Policy** (Basic Books, 1968). A more complete treatment, written more for students of social policy than for social studies teachers, is Alfred Kahn's **Theory and Practice of Social Planning** (Russell Sage, 1969). The Schorr volume is a good place to start, but serious readers will want to include the Kahn work as well. **Studies in Social Policy and Planning,** Alfred Kahn, ed. (Russell Sage, 1969), provides specific illustrations of the theories explored in the other books.

Selected Social Changes

Theories of social change are included in books mentioned elsewhere in this Guide. Readers interested in how social policy and social problems are related to social change will find the five books in this section useful. **The Triple Revolution Revisited,** Robert Perucci and Marc Pilsuk, eds. (Little, Brown, 1971, pb), is a revision of an earlier book of readings on revolutionary social trends emerging from social problems. Readers interested in cybernation, technological militarism, and human rights will find this collection comprehensive and highly readable, a good cross-section of academic and activist approaches to the future. Of particular interest to educators is Harold Hodgkinson's **Education, Interaction, and Social Change** (Prentice-Hall, 1967) which employs a systems approach to social change, emphasizing the role of education (broadly defined) as a major contributing force. The faith in policy solutions stemming from education is not carefully supported, and documentation is not at the highest level. Given these cautions, readers will find this book a unique approach to social problems and their consequences in social change.

An anthropological approach to social policy and social change is contained in Ward Goodenough's **Cooperation in Change** (Russell Sage, 1968, pb). This is an analysis of the effects of technology and modernization on social policy, especially upon underdeveloped nations. Goodenough's theory of culture and change is individualistic, as contrasted with most other theorists who see culture as existing across, rather than within, individuals. Implications for education as a function in change are implicit and thought-provoking.

There are two books which offer distinctly different analyses of society in change. Robert Angell's **Free Society and Moral Crisis** (Univ. of Michigan, 1965, pb) is representative of the more traditional structural-functionalist school, depicting society as adjusting to threats to its effective functioning, rather than requiring reorganization according to new policies based on new values. Amitai Etzioni's **The Active Society** (Free Press, 1968, pb) argues for active guidance according to certain values for the control of society. Etzioni is representative of the activist school, and this book offers support for the development of planning strategies. A reading of the two books will provide insight into the debate over functionalism and excellent perspectives on societal reactions to social problems.

Conclusion

This chapter has indicated a few outstanding books. Most of them include bibliographies for readers wanting to go further. Keeping up-to-date on social policy questions is not easy, but one periodical which is written primarily for laymen is of great help. *Social Policy*, a journal centering on policy questions, includes a variety of short articles. It can be ordered from the publisher (Suite 500, 184 Fifth Avenue, New York City). Journals devoted to specific social problems are too numerous to mention here.

22

Poverty

JAMES A. BANKS

The United States is the richest nation in the world and has attained technological advances which have been unparalleled in human history, yet there is an alarming amount of poverty amidst America's impressive affluence. In 1963, about 34.5 million Americans or 18 percent of the population were living in families which had a poverty level income and life style. Poverty is one of America's momentous social problems which must be solved if the democratic ideals upon which this nation was founded are to survive. The social studies teacher should plan units and lessons which will help students to better understand the nature of poverty in our society, and to develop the ability to make intelligent decisions so that they can take effective social action to influence public policy related to poverty. The teacher must be familiar with the nature of poverty and be able to analyze it from the perspectives of the various social sciences to successfully guide inquiry lessons. This chapter discusses resources which can help the teacher to gain a sophisticated understanding of the dimensions of poverty in American society.

Introductory Books

A review of the literature on poverty reveals an interesting trend. After the Great Depression of the 1930's waned and the prosperity of the 1950's blossomed, poor people in America were forgotten and be-

---

James A. Banks is Associate Professor of Education, University of Washington, Seattle, Washington.

came "invisible." There were few books about poverty published in the Forties and Fifties. John K. Galbraith, **The Affluent Society** (Houghton Mifflin, 1958, pb) pointed out that there was a large number of poor people within our land of prosperity. However, it was not until the publication of Michael Harrington, **The Other America: Poverty in the United States** (Penguin, 1964, pb) that a large number of American citizens and policymakers became aware of the pervasiveness of poverty in America. Harrington's book was one of the salient forces behind the "War on Poverty" which emerged in the 1960's. Another intriguing book, Sidney Lens, **Poverty: America's Enduring Paradox: A History of the Richest Nation's Unwon War** (Crowell, 1969), provides a history of poverty in America and the "wars" which have unsuccessfully tried to eliminate it. Nick Kotz, **Let Them Eat Promises: The Politics of Hunger in America** (Doubleday, 1971, pb) discusses how our failure to eliminate poverty in America has engulfed this nation in a shadow of shame. In **Rich Man, Poor Man** (Crowell, 1964), Herman P. Miller provides a highly readable analysis of the culture of poverty which exists in our affluent society.

One of the most perceptive critiques of prevailing theories of poverty and perceptions of the poor is found in Charles A. Valentine, **Culture and Poverty: Critique and Counter-Proposals** (Univ. of Chicago, 1968, pb). Ben B. Seligman's **Permanent Poverty: An American Syndrome** (Quadrangle, 1968) explores the historical and psychological factors of poverty and discusses the pervasiveness of poverty among specific sub-cultures in American society. **A Primer on the Economics of Poverty** by David Hamilton (Random House, 1968, pb) examines the meaning of poverty and makes policy recommendations for eliminating poverty in America. Alvin L. Schorr, **Poor Kids: A Report on Children in Poverty** (Basic Books, 1966) discusses the nature and characteristics of poor children and the reasons why there are large numbers of poor youths in our society.

Teachers interested in helping students to plan social action projects to eliminate poverty will find Si Kahn, **How People Get Power: Organizing Communities for Action** (McGraw-Hill, 1970) and William H. Crook and Ross Thomas, **Warriors for the Poor: The Story of VISTA** (Morrow, 1969, pb) useful. The Kahn book is a step by step outline of what to do to organize an oppressed community to obtain power. The book by Crook and Thomas is an intriguing and vivid account of the "domestic Peace Corps" which was organized to fight poverty in American communities.

Anthologies

The national focus on poverty in the 1960's is reflected in the large number of anthologies which were published during this period. Many of these books grew out of conferences sponsored by various private and public agencies. Some of these volumes are excellent because they present diverse perspectives on poverty by social scientists, journalists, public officials, and social activists.

Robert E. Will and Harold G. Vatter, **Poverty in Affluence** (Harcourt, 1965) contains readings which deal with the ideologies of poverty, poverty among different groups, and poverty as a subculture. **Poverty in America** by Margaret S. Gordan (Chandler, 1965, pb) includes an impressive collection of papers which explore problems related to the nature of poverty in the United States, views on anti-poverty programs, and suggestions for combating poverty American style. A number of essays on poverty among the aged, youths, Blacks, and Appalachian whites are found in Ben B. Seligman, **Poverty As a Public Issue** (Free Press, 1965, pb). Warner Bloomberg, Jr., and Henry J. Schmandt, **Urban Poverty: Its Social and Political Dimensions** (Russell Sage Foundation, 1968, pb) contains papers which present perspectives on institutionalized poverty in urban society, and the war on poverty as a failure in public policy. Historical views on poverty are treated in Hanna H. Meissner, **Poverty in the Affluent Society** (Harper, 1966, pb). The anthology by Louis A. Ferman, Joyce L. Kornbluh, and Alan Haber, **Poverty in America: A Book of Readings** (Univ. of Michigan, 1965, pb), consists of articles which deal with definitions of poverty, poverty and politics, and the values and life styles of the poor. A group of distinguished social scientists provides its views on American poverty in Daniel P. Moynihan, ed., **On Understanding Poverty: Perspectives from the Social Sciences** (Basic Books, 1968).

Chaim I. Waxman, **Poverty, Power and Politics** (Grosset & Dunlap, 1968, pb) includes a number of perceptive essays by social scientists, journalists, and activists on the politics of poverty. **Poverty, American Style** by Herman P. Miller (Wadsworth, 1966, pb) presents a diversity of opinions. Stimulating essays which explore questions about who are poor and why are contained in Burton A. Weisbrod, **The Economics of Poverty: An American Paradox** (Prentice-Hall, 1965, pb). The readings in Peter Townsend, **The Concept of Poverty** (American Elsevier, 1970) examine the relationship between poverty and the social structure. Alternative strategies to eliminate poverty are discussed in the Task Force on Economic Growth and Opportunity's **The Concept of Poverty** (U. S. Chamber of Commerce, 1965). The psychological effects of poverty are stressed in Vernon L. Allen, **Psychological Factors in Poverty** (Markham, 1970). The relationships between social institutions and the characteristics of poor children are treated in Nona Y. Glazer and Carol F. Creedon, **Children and Poverty: Some Sociological and Psychological Perspectives** (Rand McNally, 1968, pb). The readings in **Man Against Poverty: World War III** (Vintage, 1968, pb) by Arthur I. Blaustein and Roger R. Woock discuss the relationship between poverty and the Cold War. A number of excellent papers which challenge many traditional assumptions about language and poverty are contained in Frederick William, **Language and Poverty** (Markham, 1970). New perspectives on the life styles of the poor are presented in Eleanor B. Leacock, **The Culture of Poverty: A Critique** (Simon and Schuster, 1971).

Poverty and Race

Racism and poverty are intimately related in American society. Ethnic minority groups are disproportionately represented among the poor. Teachers interested in poverty will benefit from reading literature about racism and firsthand accounts written by individuals who have lived in poor communities. **Racism in America and How To Combat It** by the U. S. Commission on Civil Rights (USGPO, 1970) explores the nature of racism and ways to eliminate it. **The Autobiography of Malcolm X** by Malcolm X and A. Haley (Grove, 1964, pb) is a compelling and brilliant book which describes how a young man evolved from a pimp to an influential leader of his people. **Nigger: An Autobiography** by Dick Gregory and R. Lipsyte (Pocket Books, 1964, pb) relates an individual's battle with poverty and racism in Black America. Claude Brown, **Manchild in the Promised Land** (Signet, 1964, pb) sensitively recounts growing up in a black ghetto. Kenneth B. Clark, **Dark Ghetto: Dilemmas of Social Power** (Harper, 1965, pb) beautifully and poignantly describes the devastating effects of poverty on the victims of the black ghetto. James A. Banks and Jean D. Grambs, **Black Self-Concept: Implications for Education and Social Science** (McGraw-Hill, 1972) presents divergent points of view about the effects of poverty on the black child's self-concept.

The plight of the black worker is discussed in an anthology edited by Arthur M. Ross and Herbert Hill, **Employment, Race, and Poverty** (Harcourt, 1967, pb). Perceptive accounts of the poverty experienced by various ethnic groups are presented in David Gottlieb and Anne L. Heinsohn, **America's Other Youth: Growing Up Poor** (Prentice-Hall, 1971). **Black Business Enterprise: Historical and Contemporary Perspectives** (Basic Books, 1971), edited by Ronald W. Bailey, contains readings which explore the historical and contemporary perspectives of the black man's economic status in our society and suggests strategies for change. In **Future of Inequality** (Basic Books, 1970), S. M. Miller and Pamela A. Roby discuss the relationship between poverty and inequality in the distribution of income, education, social mobility, and power. The final part of the book presents proposals for social policies which can help to eliminate poverty. Whitney M. Young, Jr., in **Beyond Racism: Building An Open Society** (McGraw-Hill, 1969) outlines steps which are necessary to bring black and white America together.

23

Public Health, Especially Drugs

JAMES J. COX

Probably few problems of public health are more important to the individual and to the social structure than that of mental health. Interwoven with mental health are the use of drugs and drug abuse, twin threats to life and society. The drug problem is being studied, and dealt with, in depth by many organizations and individuals throughout the nation. Bearing on the problem of drug abuse are programs of educational prevention, institutions for inpatient and outpatient care, day and night treatment, and the use of halfway houses for the patient recovering from institutional care. There are numerous books and shorter references that deal with this subject, useful for the teacher of health and science courses in elementary and secondary schools.

A useful guide for the teacher of grades K-12 is the backbone of a study course on drugs: **Teaching about Drugs: A Curriculum Guide, K-12** (American School Health Assn., 1970). This course outline came from the Committee on Drugs of the ASHA and the Pharmaceutical Manufacturers Association. Directed at the teenager is a current paperback book by Donald J. Mercki, **Drug Abuse: Teenage Hangup.** These two books will get the teacher off to a good start in preparing for course content and orienting to the current problem in drugs.

James J. Cox is Information Officer, Public Health Service, U.S. HEW Region IV, Atlanta, Georgia.

Urgent Drug Problems

The Viet Nam war and problems of ghetto life and the urban scene have brought the problem of drugs vividly to the view of the American public. New methods of treatment are being researched in various institutions and city health centers. For example, the use of methadone in substitution for heroin is being followed in such places as the Clinical Research Center in Lexington, Kentucky, and numerous other sites located throughout the nation. Federal funds are available for treating drug users under public health laws, for staffing of dangerous drug programs, and for direct grants for special projects.

Through on-the-scene experiences in drug use and treatment, we are developing a body of literature that deals both with the use of drugs from the users' viewpoint and from the clinical reference. Richard Blum & Associates have published two volumes of intimate views of drug use: **Drugs I: Society and Drugs,** which deals with social and cultural observations; and **Drugs II: Students and Drugs,** college and high school observations (Jossey-Bass, 1969). Sidney Cohen deals with the problems that drug use has brought the user, the rationale for the user of drugs, and the roots of the flourishing of drug abuse. Cohen's book is titled **The Drug Dilemma** (McGraw-Hill, 1968).

Young people continually ask such questions as how a drug user feels — about taking drugs, his reactions to drugs, and emotions during and after taking drugs. These questions are answered in David Ebin's book called **The Drug Experience** (Grove, 1965, pb). This book has first-person accounts of addicts, writers, and scientists regarding cannabis, opium, opiates, peyote, mushrooms and LSD. It is not commonly known that "highs" or "lows" and hallucinations can be found in rather ordinary plants if one knows what to look for; mushrooms, for example. It is a dangerous game, however, for mushrooms can bring death instead of a euphoric feeling.

In the **Drug Scene: 1968** (McGraw-Hill, 1968, pb, Bantam, 1970, pb) Dr. Donald B. Louria gives a physician's clinical appraisal of drug abuse; the medical consequences and implications. Two other publications follow the pattern of clinical and critical looks at drugs: **Drugs: Facts on Their Use and Abuse,** Norman W. Houser and J. B. Richmond, (Lothrop, 1969) and the Interim Report of the Commission of Inquiry, **Non-Medical Use of Drugs** (Penguin, 1971).

Drug Groups

There is some indication that the hippie scene is passing; but the issues from that social strata still affect young people, and, indeed, the hippie lives on in slightly altered forms in communes and group living. The hippie and drugs are explored in J. D. Brown's book, **The Hippies**

(Grosset & Dunlap, 1966). Along the same lines is **Young People and Drugs** (Day, 1969) by A. H. Cain.

Hippies and drug use are fairly synonymous and in the early days of Haight-Ashbury the use of marijuana by inhabitants was taken for granted. Hard drugs were not long in coming into the picture, and before long it was generally accepted that drug users have wide-ranging tastes and appetites, including heroin, LSD, and other narcotics. Many writers spent considerable time living among the hippies and living the life of the drug user, even if a non-participating one. From close associations and friendships developed with hippies and drug users came these books: **Hippie Papers** (New American Library, 1968, pb) by Jerry Hopkins; **Hippies in Our Midst** (Fortress, 1968, pb) by L. D. Earisman; **The Hippie Trip** (Pegasus, 1968, pb) by Lewis Yablonsky; **The Hippies** (New American Library, 1968, pb) by Burton Wolfe; and **Flower People** (Ballantine, 1968, pb) by H. Gross.

College Relations

Drugs are more or less openly used on some college campuses and are not a startling revelation to many people today. Helen H. Nowlis has concluded an exhaustive appraisal of campus drug use in lay terminology which educators may find useful. The book by H. H. Nowlis, **Drugs on the College Campus** (Anchor Doubleday, 1968, pb), covers terminology, attitudes, chemistry, sociology, law, morality and education as they affect the user and society.

Almost paralleling the association of drugs with the hippie culture is the use of drugs on the campus. Most reports, however, indicate that hard drugs are in relatively small commerce in colleges, and marijuana is the principal product in use. Even so, the extent of use of the hemp plant varies widely from campus to campus, claiming only a small percentage on some campuses to, perhaps, 20 to 25 percent on others. Regular users are in considerably smaller numbers than those students who have only experimented with marijuana.

The College Drug Scene (Prentice-Hall, 1968, pb) by J. T. Carey purports to be definitive on drug users in higher education as it existed in the late 1960's. S. Pearlman is the editor of **Drugs on the Campus: Annotated Guide to the Literature** (Brooklyn Col., 1968). William Surface calls his treatment of the college class **Poisoned Ivy** (Coward-McCann, 1968). W. Young and J. Hixon limited their study to **LSD on Campus** (Dell, 1966) while Richard Blum's previously recommended books broaden the scope.

The elementary and secondary school teachers can turn to the federal government and to various health associations for publications on drugs and drug abuse. The national government has issued a pertinent health publication, **Resource Book for Drug Education** (USGPO, 1964).

The Drug Abuse Education Project of the American Association for Health, Physical Education, and Recreation, and the National Science Teachers Association developed a 117-page booklet titled, **Resource Book for Drug Abuse Education** (AAHPER, 1970, pb). And especially intended for social studies teachers is Donald J. Wolk, ed., **Drugs and Youth** (NCSS, 1971, pb), an up-to-date booklet. The National Clearinghouse for Mental Health Education prepared **Resource Book for Drug Abuse Education** and **A Federal Source Book** (Natl. Institute of Mental Health, 1969, 1970, pb).

Health in Some Social Problems

General but informative descriptions and social awareness appear in a host of publications, too many to try to include here. However, we can give examples. **Health Is a Community Affair,** National Commission on Community Health Services (Harvard Univ., 1966, pb) stresses local aspects. Another health phase is discussed in **Communicable Diseases,** D. K. Grisson, ed. (Brown, 1970, pb). B. H. Igel presents a group of six booklets, **American Health Safety Series** (Behavioral Research, 1969, pb), that deals with diseases and prevention. Perhaps more extreme, but in any case important, is Anthony Greenbank's **Book of Survival: Everyman's Guide to Staying Alive in the City, the Suburbs, and the Wild Lands** (New American, 1967, pb). Concern for current and continuing social problems beyond drugs is evidenced in Kenneth L. Jones and others, **Drugs, Alcohol, and Tobacco** (Canfield, 1970, pb).

Two health dangers also appeal widely to people. Excessive smoking or drinking may involve ill-health for some and endanger others. For publications of examples, see C. R. Carroll, **Alcohol: Use, Non-Use, and Abuse** (Brown, 1970, pb); **Alcohol and Alcoholism: Drinking and Dependence,** M. A. Black (Wadsworth, 1970, pb); and **Programmed Unit on Facts About Alcohol,** J. B. Shevlin and I. H. Goldberg (Allyn & Bacon, 1969, pb). Analogous relations involve widespread tobacco use. Samples are revealed in such publications as C. K. Kitchen, **You May Smoke** (Universal P & D, 1968); **Your Psyche: the Cigarette & the Pill** by H. E. Simmons (General Welfare, 1969); and J. C. Vermes, **Pot Is Rot and Other Horrible Facts about Bad Things** (Assn. Press, 1965, pb).

Medical and social library stacks include some difficult and some quite readable medical magazines such as *Social Casework, American Journal of Psychiatry, Clinic Toxicology, Journal of Health and Social Behavior,* and others. Besides the scattered mention of such sources, teachers may find many low or non-cost items in **Educator's Guide to Free Health, Physical Education** (Educators Progress, 1970, pb) by F. A. Horkheimer and L. E. Alley.

PART THREE

Curriculum, Methods, Media

24

Instructional Objectives and Evaluation

RALPH C. PRESTON

The spirited discussion these days about educational objectives is over how they can be formulated so as to become operational.

Ultimate Objectives

There is no dearth of excellent statements of ultimate objectives. Everybody should read the classic statement of Alfred North Whitehead in **Aims of Education** (Free Press, 1967, pb); Charles A. Beard, **A Charter for the Social Sciences in the Schools,** leading the national commission's multi-volumes of the 1930's (Scribner's, 1930's); and the President's Commission on national goals in **Goals for Americans** (Prentice-Hall, 1960). They are profound, far-reaching, and inspirational. Further labor on ultimate purposes is not needed at this juncture in time. Despite the revolutionary ideas that are sweeping the world in almost every segment of our culture, we fundamentally profess the same values that noble minds have preached for a thousand years. The above-mentioned books are useful in sharpening our sense of direction and in adding meaning to the content we teach.

It was customary a few years ago for curriculum makers and teachers to state objectives in terms of what the learner was expected to *know,* to *understand,* to *appreciate,* and to *perform.* These objectives

Ralph C. Preston is Professor of Education, Graduate School of Education, University of Pennsylvania, Philadelphia, Pennsylvania.

tended to be phrased in a general and vague manner. Typical objectives of this type were: The student should understand that the cultures of the world vary greatly. The student should see the importance of world peace. The student should be able to use map legends. The social studies curriculum guides of numerous school districts stated their objectives along these lines. Illustrations can be found in Wilhelmina Hill's **Social Studies in the Elementary School Program** (USOE, 1960, pb) and Roy A. Price's "Goals for the Social Studies" in **Social Studies Curriculum Development: Prospects and Problems** edited by Dorothy McClure Fraser (NCSS, 1969, pb). Price points out the necessity of broad general goals but he makes clear that they are not sufficient in providing guidance for the teacher and need to be supplemented with behavioral objectives.

Behavioral Objectives

The trend today is distinctly away from general objectives. In recent years teachers have been urged to create in their place objectives in behavioral terms. This means they are to identify those behaviors they expect their students to exhibit (or those tasks they expect their students to perform) following instruction—behaviors (tasks) which are observable and measurable.

Writing behavioral objectives is no easy undertaking. A teacher must know first how to distinguish general objectives from behavioral objectives. Robert F. Mager's **Preparing Instructional Objectives** (Fearon, 1962, pb) is of direct help here. It has become a classic of sorts. This little book (it contains only 60 pages), readable and programmed, takes the reader step by step into an understanding of the nature of behavioral objectives. It presents a strong case for their use in planning instruction.

Behavioral Objectives and Instruction by Robert J. Kibler and others (Allyn & Bacon, 1970, pb) is a much longer book than Mager's and its scope is broader. It contains a helpful chapter on the writing of objectives which is accompanied by programmed practice exercises for the reader. Another chapter summarizes the Bloom and the Krathwohl taxonomies of objectives which enable the teacher to formulate behavioral objectives that will cover an acceptable *range* of behaviors—from recital of factual material to the use of criteria in making evaluative judgments. Curriculum workers and teachers who are inexperienced in writing objectives of any kind, whether general or behavioral, or who do not see the relation between the two types, will find **Stating Behavioral Objectives for Classroom Instruction** by Norman E. Gronlund (Macmillan, 1970) and **Writing Behavioral Objectives: A New Approach** by H. S. McAshan (Harper & Row, 1971) particularly helpful. Either will guide them in judging the adequacy of their statements.

Perhaps no author cited in this review has done a more effective job than Robert M. Gagné in giving the underlying reasons for describing educational objectives in behavioral terms. His hard-nosed advocacy appears in **Learning and the Educational Process** edited by John D. Krumboltz (Rand McNally, 1965) and his own **The Conditions of Learning** (Holt, 1970). A recent yearbook, Lawrence E. Metcalf, ed., **Values Education: Rationale, Strategies, and Procedures** (NCSS, 1971), analyzes value objectives and presents a hypothesis on values education.

Most examples of behavioral objectives are from the fields of natural science, mathematics, and foreign language. The social studies are disappointingly neglected, probably because human performances resulting from social studies are less readily specified. By way of example, Gagné gives only a single illustration from the social studies in the two books. The social studies fare better in Paul D. Plowman's **Behavioral Objectives: Teacher Success Through Student Performances** (Science Research Associates, 1971, pb). Following a description of what is typically taught in community studies, American history, American government, and economics, Plowman lists "academic skill" objectives (such as telling within a three-minute period three rights guaranteed by the first ten amendments to the Constitution); "higher cognitive skills" objectives (such as making a mural to illustrate five ways in which the invention of the auto affected labor, consumers, and businessmen); and "creative skills" objectives (such as preparing a written plan of a model community to satisfy certain specified criteria).

Behavior Modification

One intention of many social studies teachers is to improve citizenship — not simply through supplying information *about* citizenship, but by a behavioral set toward, and participation in, affairs of school, community, conservation campaigns, and the like. Few writers have faced the full and difficult implications of transforming civic behavior. Some have simply formulated objectives in terms of verbal cognitive behavior and others have gone no further than to give vague and obscure expression to objectives of citizenship education. Teachers who earnestly desire to set objectives and plan instruction that embrace overt civic behavior should become acquainted with the literature of behavior modification. Albert Bandura's **Principles of Behavior Modification** (Holt, 1969) is probably the best work in the field. In this book, Bandura deals with modifying social behavior ranging from undesirable classroom responses (limited attention span, restlessness, hyper-aggression, and disruptive behavior) to sexual deviance and alcoholism. With praiseworthy lucidity and thoroughness, Bandura cites and interprets the relevant research findings and draws conclusions which are consistently practical and intriguing. Bandura does not, of course, try to apply the principles to social studies *per se,* but he offers guidance on how to specify objectives in ways that could be used by teachers in planning programs for inculcating aspects of citizenship.

Critiques of Behavioral Objectives

Despite the logical case that has been made for behavioral objectives, not all educators and psychologists embrace them as a helpful or necessary solution to the curriculum-evaluation problem. One skeptical view is found in **The Process of Schooling: A Psychological Examination** by J. M. Stephens (Holt, 1967).

Another critical view of a different sort is presented by Philip W. Jackson in **Life in Classrooms** (Holt, 1968). He analyzes the "engineering point of view" which he contends has created the movement to have objectives stated in behavioral terms. Jackson believes the major weakness of the approach when applied to elementary schools, at least, is its oversimplified image of what goes on in the classroom.

He also illustrates ways in which teachers are intuitively more behaviorally oriented than they are often given credit for. Their chief contribution, he believes, lies in their ability to convince students that the compulsory activities that face them are worthwhile, and that what they are doing is not just busy-work. One of the giants of modern educational psychology, David P. Ausubel, takes the position that to exhort curriculum workers to state their objectives as behaviors "often does more harm than good" in **Educational Psychology: A Cognitive View** (Holt, 1968). He fears that it may lead curriculum workers to "give more attention to relatively trivial but readily definable goals than to goals that are intrinsically more important but resistive to precise behavioral definition." Probably most social studies teachers would agree. Behavioral objectives can at best account for but a small portion of the anticipated outcomes of social studies instruction.

Rebuttal by Exponents of Behavioral Objectives

Kibler and others add a postscript to their volume consisting of a paper by W. James Popham who responds to eleven criticisms of behavioral objectives. Popham makes it apparent that some of the criticisms are superficial, but to this reviewer, his rebuttal to some of the more significant accusations is weak. For example, to the contention that constructing behavioral objectives is difficult and would require an excessive amount of the teacher's time, he offers the quixotic solution: "We must reduce public school teaching loads to those of college professors." A more sophisticated and satisfactory handling of the criticism is by Gagné in the Krumboltz book. Bandura takes up at length and with fairness (though from a behavior-oriented bias) the charge that proponents of behavior modification are authoritarian manipulators of other human beings.

Objectives and Evaluation

All the foregoing books treat the role of behavioral objectives in offering a valid foundation for evaluation. If the objectives have been worded as suggested by Gagné so as to contain overt action ("state," "derive," "identify," etc.), then what could be more logical or fitting than to have the evaluation based entirely on the student's ability at the end of a unit to perform each of these actions? Mager supplies a vivid illustration. He states immediately the behaviors he expects the reader to perform upon completion of the book. At the end of the book he gives an objective test which calls for those behaviors to be performed. Unfortunately, because his objectives and test items are limited to Bloom's lowest category, knowledge, many readers have no doubt come to the conclusion, as Kibler and his associates point out, that behavioral objectives must be shallow. It is unfortunate that a yearbook of NCSS, **Evaluation in Social Studies,** edited by Harry D. Berg (NCSS, 1965), which devotes considerable space to objectives and evaluation in the social studies, does not really lock horns with the central issue which the aforementioned authors have raised. The yearbook is helpful, however, in providing leads on how to construct objective test items, how to evaluate critical thinking in the social studies, how to improve the essay test in the social studies, and in listing available published tests. And a new edition has appeared of **Selected Items for the Testing of Study Skills and Critical Thinking** (NCSS, 1971, pb), a bulletin by Horace Morse and George McCune and revised by Lester Brown and Ellen Cook. Here are practical ways that test students' development of critical thinking abilities.

Critical reviews of 16 social studies tests and specialized tests in the various social sciences will be found in **The Sixth Mental Measurements Yearbook** edited by Oscar K. Buros (Gryphon, 1965). The utility of the procedures and tests discussed in the three books just mentioned is enhanced by their not being limited to the narrow approach of the behavioral cult.

Looming large in evaluation today is the National Assessment Project, designed to develop tests that reflect national objectives. Results of its pilot tryout in civics are given in **Citizenship: National Results — Partial,** National Assessment of Educational Progress Report No. 2 (Education Commission of the States, Denver, 1970). For a critical and lively discussion of national assessment and its related concept, accountability, see **Proceedings of the 1970 Invitational Conference on Testing Problems,** Gene V. Glass, chairman (Educational Testing Service, 1971).

25

General Instruction and Resources

W. WILLIAMS STEVENS, JR.

This chapter attempts to describe sources of information available in two major categories of social studies education: general readings for social studies teachers, and instructional materials and realia for students at the elementary and secondary levels. The general readings section is an effort to give teachers a feeling for the new social studies materials which were developed primarily during the 1960's. The brief notations at the end of this chapter on instructional materials are suggestions for further investigation on the part of interested readers.

General Readings

Although Jerome Bruner has recently voiced some reservations about intellectual positions which he had championed during the early 1960's, his works stand as some of the most important contributions to the new social studies literature. In particular, **The Process of Education** (Vintage, 1960), a delightful book published in 1960 as a result of a conference at Woods Hole, served as the inspiration for much of the curriculum materials development in the Sixties.

Two other conferences, both supported by the U.S. Office of Education, produced works that are important in understanding the origins of what is described as the new social studies movement. In 1963 the Cubberly Conference at Stanford University produced **Social Studies:**

W. Williams Stevens, Jr., is Associate Director, Social Science Education Consortium. This chapter was prepared with the assistance of John D. Haas, Director, Center for Education in the Social Sciences, and Jack E. Cousins, Professor of Education, University of Colorado, Boulder, Colorado.

Curriculum Proposals for the Future (Scott, Foresman, 1963), edited by G. Wesley Sowards. Later a conference held at Syracuse University resulted in the National Council for the Social Studies Research Bulletin, **Needed Research in the Teaching of the Social Studies** (NCSS, 1964, pb) edited by Roy Price, which seemed to give the impetus to further research and examination of social studies curricula. Another relevant work is Leonard S. Kenworthy, **Background Papers for Social Studies Teachers** (Wadsworth, 1966, pb).

In 1962, a combined effort of the American Council of Learned Societies resulted in **Social Studies and the Social Sciences,** edited by Bernard Berelson (Harcourt, 1962). This volume opened the door to the investigation of concepts and structures in the social science disciplines and their usefulness in social studies curricula. Two other books exemplify this focus on structure and concepts: **Concepts and Structures in the New Social Science Curricula** (Holt, 1967) edited by Irving Morrissett, and **Education and the Structure of Knowledge** (Rand McNally, 1964) edited by Stanley Elam. Particular attention should be centered on Chapter One in the Elam book, written by Joseph Schwab, which deals with discipline structure as a tool for curriculum development. James G. Womack, **Discovering the Structure of Social Studies** (Benziger, 1966) deals with social studies generalizations, an interdisciplinary approach to generalization, and a plan of action for developing a K-12 social studies program.

Many of these early writers were not in education but instead represented specific disciplines. Arthur R. King, Jr., and John A. Brownell, **The Curriculum and the Disciplines of Knowledge** (Wiley, 1966), and Philip H. Phenix, **Realms of Meaning** (McGraw-Hill, 1964) were among the first educators to write on the relationship of the structures of knowledge to curriculum building. In 1969 William Lowe edited **Structure and the Social Studies** (Cornell Univ., 1969), a volume which grew out of a series of curriculum workshops at Cornell University. **Concepts and Structure in the New Social Science Curricula** (Holt, 1967, pb), edited by Irving Morrissett, discusses the relationship between substantive content, learning processes, and values. It presents many of the aspects which have precipitated the "revolution in social studies."

Forerunners of the Movement

The new social studies movement, like most intellectual reform movements, has its forerunners who were re-discovered and popularized as the movement gained impetus. Many of the curriculum developers of the Sixties found useful insights in the writings of John Dewey, **How We Think** (Heath, 1933) and Charles A. Beard, **The Nature of the Social Sciences** (Scribner's, 1934). From Dewey came the basis for the teaching of process or mode of inquiry, and from Beard the notion that all the social sciences could form the superstructure upon which social studies curricula could be built.

Trends in the New Social Studies Movement

A number of trends can be detected in the new social studies. Two schools of thought seemed to pervade the curriculum. The "majority party" were those who drew their emphasis from the nature of knowledge, perceiving structures of knowledge, the "high-mileage" concepts, and from the ways of producing knowledge (the methodologies) used by the practitioners of the disciplines. The edited work by Morrissett is one which exemplifies this trend; another work of the "majority party" was a small book edited by G. W. Ford and L. Pugno, **Structure of Knowledge and Curriculum** (Rand McNally, 1964).

The "minority party" derived its thrusts from the nature of society and from the nature of generalized thought processes. They advocated an approach which would focus student interest on contemporary (though not transient) social issues which dominate public policy debate. Some books which are helpful in understanding how this group of curriculum scholars dealt with this sensitive area include: H. G. Hullfish and Philip G. Smith, **Reflective Thinking: The Method of Education** (Dodd, Mead, 1961); Maurice P. Hunt and Lawrence E. Metcalf, **Teaching High School Social Studies** (Harper & Row, 1968); Donald W. Oliver and James P. Shaver, **Teaching Public Issues in the High School** (Houghton Mifflin, 1966); James P. Shaver and Harold Berlak, eds., **Democracy, Pluralism, and the Social Studies** (Houghton Mifflin, 1968); and Fred Newmann and Donald Oliver, **Clarifying Public Controversy** (Little, Brown, 1970).

Interesting for discussion and analysis are R. E. Gross and R. H. Muessig, eds., **Problem-Centered Social Studies Instruction: Approaches to Reflective Teaching** (NCSS, 1971, pb); Abraham Kaplan, **Conduct of Inquiry: Methodology for Behavioral Science** (Chandler, 1964, pb); and Barry K. Beyer and Anthony N. Penna, eds., **Concepts in the Social Studies** (NCSS, 1971, pb).

During the last half of the decade of the Sixties, many educational leaders began to realize that the curriculum reform movement had neglected several crucial areas. One neglected area is the affective domain—values, value analysis and the feelings of persons toward each other.

Publications in the affective area or domain include books by Neil Postman and Charles Weingartner, **Teaching as a Subversive Activity** (Delacorte, 1969); Robert F. Mager, **Developing Attitudes Toward Learning** (Fearon, 1968); Richard M. Jones, **Fantasy and Feeling in Education** (New York Univ., 1968); Terry Borton, **Reach, Touch, and Teach** (McGraw-Hill, 1970); Gerald Weinstein and Mario Fantini, **Toward**

Humanistic Education: A Curriculum of Affect (Praeger, 1970); Carl Rogers, **Freedom to Learn** (Merrill, 1969); and Kenneth E. Eble, **A Perfect Education** (Macmillan, 1966).

New Media of Social Studies in the 1970's

Many of the new materials which are now commercially available contain a number of simulations and simulation games. Teachers find these activities rewarding as teaching tools, and students often find them interesting and involving. Two of the best and most recent books reflecting the significance of their use are William A. Nesbitt, **Simulation Games for the Social Studies Classroom** (Foreign Policy Association, 1971), and a prior volume, **Simulation Games in Learning** edited by S. S. Boocock and E. O. Schild (Russell Sage Foundation, 1968), which is an excellent introduction to the development of the simulation movement. Both contain materials on the design of, and research on, using simulations.

Classroom questioning has become a major tool for teachers to develop inquiry skills in students. A useful work which deals with the techniques of classroom questioning is Norris M. Sanders' **Classroom Questions: What Kind?** (Harper & Row, 1966). Also parts of Edwin Fenton's **The New Social Studies** (Holt, 1967, pb) deal with the use of questioning techniques in stimulating inquiry.

Curriculum and Assessment

Another part of the literature of the new social studies movement is the curriculum materials development project directories. Social Science Education Consortium (SSEC) distributes the **Social Studies Curriculum Materials Data Book** (SSEC, 1971) which contains descriptions and abstracts of virtually all major social studies projects. The work serves as both a directory and a source of vital data on each project. Other available directories include the Association of Supervision and Curriculum Development's **Social Studies Education Projects: An ASCD Index** compiled by Bob L. Taylor and Thomas L. Groom (NEA, 1971); and **Marin County Social Studies Project Directory** by G. Sidney Lester and David Bond (Marin County Public Schools, 1970). The latter directory can be found in the ERIC collection.

Also most state departments of education have published directories of projects — especially thorough are the ones published by Pennsylvania and Texas. *Social Education* (vol. 34, No. 4) contains "A Critical Appraisal of Twenty-Six National Social Studies Projects," edited by Norris M. Sanders and Marlin L. Tanck. Also significant is Frederick Risinger and Michael Radz, **Social Studies Projects Tour** (SSEC & ERIC

ChESS, 1971, pb). The authors were members of a group of SSEC teacher associates who visited and reported on 24 major social studies projects.

It is not feasible to list in this chapter all student curriculum materials which have been produced during the past ten years that could be considered part of the new social studies. These materials represent broadly social science disciplines as well as social issues approaches. There are many recent attempts to produce interdisciplinary and multidisciplinary curricula. There are also several packages which deal with current issues and use the social science disciplines as supporting tools but not as the major focus.

At least two developers have worked during the past decade on developing analytical instruments to be used in describing and evaluating curriculum materials. These developers are the Social Science Education Consortium and Alan Tom of Washington University. **The Curriculum Materials Analysis System** by Irving Morrissett and W. Williams Stevens, Jr., of the SSEC is still available from the Consortium (SSEC, 1967), and the publication by Alan Tom is **An Approach to Selecting Among Social Studies Curricula** (CMREL, 1970). Products of these evaluations can be of assistance to curriculum decision-makers who select materials for classroom use.

Conclusion

Methods textbooks in social studies education are often not only for use in training prospective and/or experienced teachers. Their use in college courses and in school system instruction of teachers has widely expanded curriculum and methods in social studies in the 1960's and 1970's. Most of these textbooks are generally classified as either for elementary or secondary teachers. A variety of each type of textbook will be cited in other chapters.

26

Elementary Schools' Teaching and Learning

JOHN R. LEE

My daughters used to chat a ditty about a little girl with a curl in the middle of her forehead. The ditty ended with: "When she was good, she was very, very good; but when she was bad, she was horrid." That's the way it was with elementary social studies in the sixth decade of this century. When it was good, it *was* very, very good, but when it was bad, it was *horrid*. Everyone argued over purposes, teachers worried about their background in the social sciences, developmental psychology resurfaced, bandwagons clattered through our journals, publishers began to invest in new series and media, and the voices of concepts, structure, and inquiry were heard throughout the land.

These background ideas are dealt with at length elsewhere in this volume, but among the more useful publications are several that deal with elementary and other grade levels regarding social studies. Authors cited include Muessig and Rogers; Beyer and Penna; Womack; Herbert and Murphy; Allen; Gross, McPhie and Fraenkel; and multi-authors in an ACLS/NCSS book.

Methods Textbooks

Three of the more widely used methods books in the Sixties dealt with nearly the full range of topics from goals to tests, and each had something to say on almost everything. John Jarolimek's **Social Studies**

John R. Lee is Professor of Education, School of Education, Northwestern University, Evanston, Illinois.

in Elementary Education (Macmillan, 1971) translates theory into explanations and illustrations satisfying to most teachers. John Michaelis' **Social Studies for Children in a Democracy** (Prentice-Hall, 1968) strikes a response with teachers for its attention to details; if you want to know how to organize a unit, make a map, or select films, this book provides clear examples and practical suggestions. Ralph Preston's **Teaching Social Studies in the Elementary School** (Holt, 1968) focuses on the preparation of four types of units, each clearly and amply described. He provides a superior section on the use of reading in social studies.

Lavona Hanna, Neva Hagaman, and Gladys Potter's **Unit Teaching in the Elementary School** (Holt, 1963) remains *the* basic text on the teaching of units through the use of units, dramatic play, and construction in the classroom. Edith Merritt's **Working With Children in Social Studies** (Wadsworth, 1961) also stresses the uses of units and dramatic play.

In some respects, two books laid the foundation for a shift from the old to the new social studies. William Ragan and John McAulay's **Social Studies for Today's Children** (Appleton, 1964) and Bruce Joyce's **Strategies for Elementary Social Science Education** (Science Research Assn., 1965) expressed a general dissatisfaction with old programs and orthodox methods, and each laid out some new directions for the late Sixties.

Three books characterized by general how-to-do-it sections came out in the Sixties. W. Linwood Chase wrote **A Guide for the Elementary Social Studies Teacher** (Allyn & Bacon, 1966, pb), a product of his years of practical experience. James A. Smith stressed creativity and provided checklists for nearly everything in his **Creative Teaching of the Social Studies in the Elementary School** (Allyn & Bacon, 1967, pb). Leonard Kenworthy led the early fight for understanding other peoples and their cultures; his **Social Studies for the Seventies** (Ginn, 1969, pb) reflects his early interests and appeals to outward-looking undergraduates. Malcolm Douglass' **Social Studies: From Theory to Practice in Elementary Education** (Lippincott, 1967) deals particularly well with approaches to organizing social studies programs. Edgar Wesley and William Cartwright revised **Teaching Social Studies in Elementary Schools** (Heath, 1968). Wesley worked with concepts before most of us gave them a thought, and Cartwright knows more about U.S. history than thee or me; this is a book by wise men.

Several books laid stress on problem solving and inquiry. Maxine Dunfee and Helen Sagl's **Social Studies Through Problem Solving** (Holt, 1966) brought teachers a new look at pupil-teacher planning and problem-solving. **Social Study: Inquiry in the Elementary Classroom** (Bobbs-Merrill, 1966) by Millard Clements, William Fielder, and Robert Tabachnick combines the notions of inquiry, the social sciences, and concern for the child; undergraduates respond especially well to this book's descriptions of inquiry. Richard Servey's **Social Studies Instruction in the Elementary School** (Chandler, 1967) provides excellent examples of guiding children into and closing inquiry; it includes a fine discussion of the development of the new social studies. Hilda Taba's **Teacher's Handbook for Elementary Social Studies** (Addison-Wesley, 1969, pb) describes and illustrates her ideas about reasoning and contains strategies for the development of thought processes used in value analysis. **New Approaches to Teaching Elementary Social Studies** (Burgess, 1969) by Donald Barnes and Arlene Burgdorf contains many fine ideas on inquiry, including some interesting exercises for evaluating the ability to generalize. Bernice Goldmark's **Social Studies: A Method of Inquiry** (Wadsworth, 1968) brings a hard-nosed touch of philosophical analysis to elementary social studies. Its five-stage model of inquiry won't suit all teachers, but those who wish to stress reasoning as a goal should read this book.

With the confusion over the "new" social studies, books of readings gained popularity in the late Sixties. Jonathon McLendon and William Joyce (with John R. Lee) published **Readings on Elementary Social Studies** (Allyn & Bacon, 1970, pb), and John Jarolimek and Huber Walsh's **Readings for Social Studies in Elementary Education** (Macmillan, 1969, pb) also appeared. A collection of *Social Education* articles was presented in **An Anthology of Readings in Elementary Social Studies,** edited by Huber M. Walsh (NCSS, 1971). It contains selected articles published by the most recognized national organization exclusively in this field.

Potpourri

Among the special methods, Fannie and George Shaftel's **Role-Playing for Social Values** (Prentice-Hall, 1967) has become a classic in its own time. Wayne Herman edited **Current Research in Elementary School Social Studies** (Macmillan, 1969, pb); some articles provide enough information on practices to help a teacher with decisions about her own classroom, but the reader should remember that small group research results cannot always be generalized to all other groups of children. Maxine Dunfee's **Elementary School Social Studies: A Guide to Current Research** (ASCD, 1970, pb) and Jonathon McLendon and F. C. Penix's **What Research Says to the Teacher: Teaching the Social Studies** (NEA, 1968, pb) are other worthwhile sources of information on research.

Several new books on elementary social studies have been published. The format of Frank L. Ryan's **Exemplars for the New Social Studies** (Prentice-Hall, 1971) almost forces the reader to work in an inquiry mode while considering teaching components of elementary social studies. R. Murray Thomas and Dale L. Brubaker contend and illustrate in **Decisions in Teaching Elementary Social Studies** (Wadsworth, 1971) that the quality of a teacher's decisions on objectives, method, and evaluation determine the quality of his social studies teaching. Dorothy J. Skeel's **The Challenge of Teaching Social Studies in the Elementary School** (Goodyear, 1970) describes problem-solving through inquiry, unit teaching, and structure as method. The treatment of values, value analysis, and religion as part of the social studies curriculum is unique in Milton E. Ploghoft and Albert H. Shuster's **Social Science Education in the Elementary School** (Merrill, 1971). Focusing the arts, humanities, and the social sciences on the overarching idea of the world community is the theme of **The World: Context for Teaching in the Elementary School,** by Edith W. King (Brown, 1971). To the writer's knowledge the first to focus exclusively on this topic, R. Murray Thomas and Dale L. Brubaker's **Curriculum Patterns in Elementary Social Studies** (Wadsworth, 1971) describes and evaluates privately published programs and the major funded curriculum projects.

What books are needed in the early Seventies? Most desirable would be a book on objectives and evaluation with examples for every elementary grade; several books on ethnic groups and social studies; a series of Shaftel-type role-playing books on case studies, gaming, and sources; and a few methods books where authors take controversial positions on any number of topics.

27

Secondary Schools' Teaching and Learning

WILLIAM B. FINK

The social studies pot began to boil in the 1960's. The curriculum revolutions that had earlier been experienced by foreign languages, the natural sciences, and English hit the social studies in this decade. Beginning with Project Social Studies of the United States Office of Education in 1963 Federal funds began to flow in appreciable amount to this previously neglected field. Curriculum centers around the country spearheaded curriculum reform, the production of new materials, and inservice programs for teachers. The production of books and articles increased dramatically, particularly after 1965. Various authors analyzed the provocative views of Jerome Bruner concerning the "structure" of the disciplines and applied them to methods of secondary social studies instruction.

There were explorations of Bruner's ideas by William T. Lowe, **Structure and the Social Studies** (Cornell, 1969), which reports the results of a series of workshops in which practicing teachers and discipline specialists studied the curriculum revision movement.

Educational journals published vast numbers of articles about the Bruner thesis. A useful collection of the most valuable is Louis J. Hebert and William Murphy, eds., **Structure in the Social Studies.** A companion volume, **Inquiry in the Social Studies,** is edited by Rodney Allen, John Fleckenstein, and Peter Lyon (both NCSS, 1968, pb).

One of the most prominent supporters of an "inquiry" approach is Edwin Fenton, Director of the Social Studies Project at Carnegie Mellon

---

William B. Fink is Chairman of the Department of Social Science Education and Professor of History at State University College at Oneonta, New York.

University. His **Teaching the New Social Studies in Secondary Schools** (Holt, 1966, pb) is a different kind of methods book. Fenton's **The New Social Studies** (Holt, 1967, pb) is an overall view of what the movement is all about. In 1965-66 he visited some social studies curriculum projects throughout the country. He summarized what was going on, with examples, under these headings: Objectives and Evaluation, Teaching Strategies, Materials, Pupil Deployment, and Teacher Preparation. A book with the same title, **The New Social Studies** (Peacock, 1970, pb) by Mark M. Krug and others makes critical evaluations of the new materials produced by some of the leading social studies projects. These stress secondary more than elementary social studies project reports.

A number of authors responded to the need of teachers for help in teaching the "New Social Studies" by producing "new" method texts. In 1955 Maurice P. Hunt and Lawrence E. Metcalf foreshadowed aspects of the current social studies movement in **Teaching High School Social Studies** (Harper, 1968). They emphasized "reflective thinking," essentially the scientific approach to solving problems.

Going somewhat beyond this, Byron G. Massialas and C. Benjamin Cox, in **Inquiry in Social Studies** (McGraw-Hill, 1966), consider "the method of inquiry as being the only appropriate and productive approach to social studies teaching."

Mark Krug, a mature scholar, disputes this view. He points out some of the difficulties of the advocates of the "new" social studies in **History and the Social Sciences** (Blaisdell, 1967). He sees it as *one* useful method. Furthermore, Krug questions Bruner's "structure of disciplines" approach and doubts that scholars can agree on the structure of most disciplines.

In one of the significant works of the past ten years, Donald W. Oliver and James P. Shaver, **Teaching Public Issues in the High School** (Houghton Mifflin, 1966, pb), the authors also deny the value of the structure approach to the curriculum. Almost alone among the current curriculum designers, these authors, who were both connected with the Harvard Social Studies Project, base their approach on a philosophy of the social order.

While advocates of "new" social studies pushed their views, some time-tested methods texts continued to serve the teachers. Over the years no text has been more popular than Edgar B. Wesley and Stanley P. Wronski, **Teaching Social Studies in High School** (Heath, 1964), to be published in a revised edition early in the 1970's. Useful and practical is Jonathon C. McLendon, **Social Studies in Secondary Education** (Macmillan, 1965). Gerald Leinwand and Daniel M. Feins, **Teaching History and the Social Studies in Secondary Schools** (Pitman, 1968) is geared to the beginning teacher in an urban school. Old, but still useful, are Dorothy McClure Fraser and Edith West, **Social Studies in Secondary Schools** (Ronald, 1961), and Morris R. Lewenstein, **Teaching Social Studies in Junior and Senior High Schools** (Rand McNally, 1963). Richard

E. Gross, Jack Fraenkel, and Walter McPhie published a volume of popular readings, **Teaching the Social Studies** (Intext, 1969).

During the 1960's numbers of practical, down-to-earth books aimed directly at the classroom came from the presses. The American Council of Learned Societies and the National Council for the Social Studies collaborated on **The Social Studies and the Social Sciences** (Harcourt, 1962), and Erling Hunt edited **High School Social Studies Perspectives** (Houghton Mifflin, 1962, pb).

Under the editorship of Erling Hunt, Teachers College, Columbia University, publishes a useful series of small books entitled **Social Studies Sources.** In **Honors Teaching in American History** (Teachers College, 1969), Laurence Fink describes his experience teaching an honors course in suburban New York. A source of ideas is Donald W. Robinson, in collaboration with others, **Promising Practices in Civic Education** (NCSS, 1967, pb). The project members of this survey supported by the Danforth Foundation visited 83 selected schools in 27 states.

Year after year the National Council for the Social Studies provides first-rate materials for practicing teachers. Their widely distributed books concentrate often on social science disciplines, reported in other chapters. Other volumes of the yearbooks often stress social studies secondary teachers' special interests. Helen McCracken Carpenter produced **Skill Development in Social Studies** (NCSS, 1963, pb). The subject of evaluation receives thorough treatment in Harry D. Berg, ed., **Evaluation in Social Studies;** editors Jean Fair and Fannie R. Shaftel have collaborated on **Effective Thinking in the Social Studies;** and Dorothy McClure Fraser edited a useful book, **Social Studies Curriculum Developments: Prospects and Problems** (all NCSS, 1963, 1965, 1967, 1969, pb).

The National Council's Curriculum Series contains specific suggestions for courses of study. The following deal specifically with the secondary level: **Social Studies for Young Adolescents: Programs for Grades 7, 8, 9,** Julian C. Aldrich and Eugene Cottle, eds.; **Social Studies in the High School: Programs for Grades Ten, Eleven, and Twelve,** Willis D. Moreland, ed.; and **Social Studies in Transition: Guidelines for Change,** Dorothy McClure Fraser and Samuel P. McCutchen, eds. (NCSS, 1967, 1965, 1965, pb).

Recently the Social Science Education Consortium and ERIC ChESS (Boulder, Colorado) continued recording and producing useful materials. **Social Studies Curriculum Materials Data Book** (SSEC, 1971, plus supplements) is designed to help teachers evaluate and select materials for their classrooms. This loose-leaf volume which is updated periodically contains analyses of new teaching materials that appear on the market. The book is offered on a subscription basis.

Even this cursory survey of the recent literature reinforces the view that the social studies field is where the action is. One thing seems certain: the "New Social Studies" movement is only beginning. Major changes lie ahead, continuing as well as often stretching beyond secondary social studies education.

28

General Colleges and Universities

RICHARD WHITTEMORE AND DANIEL J. SORRELLS

Educational warfare rages all around social studies teachers today, but they are often removed from the action. While decisive battles are fought on college campuses and in the streets, teachers along with nearly everyone else in the educational establishment have become semi-displaced persons. The process of educational decision-making is being de-professionalized with consequences that are as yet only dimly perceived. Accountability has become the watchword of all education. For the moment, at least, one cannot expect much illumination from the professional literature. There are, however, commonly inspired kinds of writings concerning the university and its purposes which may help social science educators better understand the role of higher education in a time of rapid change.

The liberal tradition in higher education was an early casualty of mass education and the machine age. Today it is practically extinct except in the minds of a few professional types who harbor some "old hat" notions about the importance of a cultural heritage. Academia did not give up easily, however. In the 1930's Robert M. Hutchins made an eloquent plea for the restoration of humanistic education in **Higher Learning in America** (Yale Univ., 1936, pb), yet his metaphysical yearnings for ultimates did not suit the pragmatic temper of modern America. More realistically, the Harvard faculty sought a compromise between general and special education. Its **General Education in a Free Society** (Harvard Univ., 1945) is a classic of sorts. A more hardheaded

---

Richard Whittemore is Professor of History, Teachers College, Columbia University, New York. Daniel J. Sorrells is Professor of Higher Education, College of Education, University of Georgia, Athens, Georgia.

vision of the role of the university appeared in Clark Kerr's **Uses of the University** (Harvard Univ., 1963, pb). Then president of the University of California, Kerr wrote of his experience in that vast educational complex and gave us the term "multiversity." He did not invent the frightening impersonality of this Leviathan, but he seemed to accept it as inevitable.

"Multiversity" quickly became a code word for all the ills of higher education. One university's attempt to diagnose and prescribe for its problems was **The Reforming of General Education** by the Columbia sociologist Daniel Bell (Columbia Univ., 1966, pb). Bell's brilliant report proposed that the college be put back at the center of the university's intellectual life. With a truly liberal curriculum it would give first priority to the development of intellectual independence, to the *how* of knowing rather than the *what.* However, it assigns a purely preparatory role to the secondary school. Jacques Barzun, also of Columbia, in **American University: How It Runs, Where It Is Going** (Harper & Row, 1968, pb), gloomily predicted the early demise of the American college as we know it unless the liberal arts become its focus once again. A more likely issue, he concluded, will be the amalgamation of the last two years of high school and the first two years of college creating a kind of school for general studies to fill the void between grammar and graduate training.

And then came the "revolution" at Columbia. In April 1968, the young rebels hurled "non-negotiable demands" at the feet of a befuddled administration and, though begging all the questions, forced a reappraisal of the whole university system. It all began at Berkeley in 1964, and as the agonies of Columbia, Harvard, and Yale followed in 1968, 1969, and 1970, a voluminous literature on student protest appeared. Companion pieces on the University of California "Free Speech Movement" are S. M. Lipset and S. S. Wolin, eds., **The Berkeley Student Revolt** (Doubleday, 1965, pb) and C. G. Katope and P. Zolbrod, **Beyond Berkeley: A Source Book in Student Values** (World Publishing Co., 1966, pb). Two important and quite different views of the Columbia uprising may be found in the Cox Commission's report, **Crisis at Columbia** (Vintage, 1968, pb) and Jerry Avorn, **Up Against the Ivy Wall** (Atheneum, 1969, pb). The Commission headed by Professor Archibald Cox of the Harvard Law School made its investigation at the behest of the Columbia Faculties Executive Committee and with the blessing of the administration. Avorn was an editor of the *Columbia Daily Spectator* during the time of troubles, and **Up Against the Ivy Wall** is his and his fellow editors' accounts of what happened.

A careful study of the Harvard affair of 1969 is L. E. Eichel and others, **Harvard Strike** (Houghton Mifflin, 1970, pb), while a moving account of one student's experiences during the disturbances is Richard Zorza, **The Right to Say "We"** (Praeger, 1970). The crisis at Yale was in some ways the most threatening of all, connected as it was with the opening of the New Haven Black Panther trials. The fact that there was no serious violence is quite remarkable, as John Hersey's warm and sympathetic **Letter to the Alumni** (Knopf, 1970) makes clear.

Two fascinating collections of essays on student protest are to be found in special issues of *The American Scholar* (Autumn, 1969), and *The Annals of the American Academy of Political and Social Science* (May, 1971). Of special interest is an analysis of Edgar Friedenberg's. He does not see high school difficulties as entirely homologous to college and university problems. Probably the best statement of the liberal faculty position regarding student activism in university affairs is the Columbia philosopher Charles Frankel's **Education and the Barricades** (Norton, 1968, pb). Newly returned from service in the United States Department of State, Frankel found his university in disarray; this is his analysis of the situation and its significance.

For an exact historical focus, an indispensable reference work is R. Hofstadter and W. Smith, **American Higher Education: A Documentary History** (Univ. of Chicago, 1961, pb), a two-volume anthology of selected writings. Perhaps the best single publication for providing a panoramic overview of the development and growth of higher education as a major contribution to our society is **Higher Education in Transition** by John S. Brubacher and Willis Rudy (Harper & Row, 1968). It is a scholarly written text which provides a wealth of background information for understanding the present status of college and university life.

Two important recent publications which give perspective to the multiplicity of problems — social, educational, and financial — faced by colleges today and which offer some pertinent suggestions toward their solution are Algo D. Henderson, **The Innovative Spirit** (Jossey-Bass, 1970), a delightfully written book by one of today's foremost leaders in higher education, and **Search for Relevance** by Axelrod, *et al.* (Jossey-Bass, 1969).

For those whose interests lie in the two-year institution, usually designated the junior college but more recently expanded into the community college, there are B. Lamar Johnson, **Islands of Innovation Expanding: Changes in the Community College** (Glencoe, 1969) and **This Is the Community College** (Houghton Mifflin, 1968, pb) by Edmund J. Gleazer. James W. Thornton, Jr., **The Community Junior College** (Wiley, 1966) offers an approach to understanding the changing role of this facet of higher education.

Overlooked, insufficiently researched areas of higher education are those of curriculum and instruction. A new important contribution to this field is the publication by Paul Dressel, **College and University Curriculum** (McCutchan, 1971). Excellent bibliographical listings at the end of each chapter provide sources of further exploration. Joseph J. Schwab in his **College Curriculum and Student Protest** (Univ. of Chicago, 1969, pb) vividly points up the relationships of academic program requirements, methods by which courses are taught on most campuses, as a prime source of concern and discontent by students who feel "trapped" by academic requirements which fail to meet their educational expectations or personal needs. For a better understanding of the role of the student in relation to his total campus environment, **The College and the Student** edited by Lawrence Dennis and Joseph Kauffman (American Council on Education, 1966) provides keen insights from many sources.

A guide for finding what was published in 1969-70 related to higher education is Lewis B. Mayhew, **The Literature in Higher Education** (Jossey-Bass, 1971). The author categorizes recent writings into nine areas, briefly annotates each one, and cites his personal reactions to their content. Whether or not one agrees with Mayhew's analyses, the volume is a valuable ready reference. Two additional references, among many which might be suggested for providing added dimension to one's understanding of the changing role of higher education, would include Russell L. Acoff, "Toward an Idealized University," appearing in the December 1968 issue of *Management Science,* and the refreshing and provocative book by Otto Butz, ed., **To Make a Difference** (Harper, 1967).

As recently as two years ago one might have asked, "What have all the problems of higher education to do with the elementary and secondary schools?" Today social studies teachers do not need to be told that the upheavals rocking college campuses are simply more spectacular manifestations of the turbulence they find in their own classrooms. They know that not only the colleges, but the whole educational world has been boosted into a new orbit. All the shoptalk of the 1960's about the "new social studies," "the structure of knowledge," and "discovery learning," important as it was, suddenly seems to belong to another lifetime. The crisis of our society has taken hold of the minds of students and it is the social studies teacher who is most affected. He above all others in the schools should be sensitive to students' concerns and be able to help them direct their dissatisfactions toward positive goals.

PART FOUR

Perspectives on Human Development

29

Child Culture

EVERETT T. KEACH, JR.

The subculture of childhood is being subjected to an intensive investigation in this century. The rapidly expanding knowledge base of every aspect of the child's development is generating heated controversy about the relationships that should exist between the child and the adult in our society. As we experiment with new patterns for formalizing the structure of the child's experiences, we are adding immeasurably to our knowledge of the social, emotional and intellectual variables which make up the context of childhood. Programs such as Headstart, Follow Through, and the Open Classrooms are discussed by educators and laymen alike. The demand for knowledge to help the adult understand the child is also being precipitated by our awareness of the changing function of the family, the increasing dependence upon television as a communication medium, increasing ease of living, to name a few variables.

A General Introduction to Child Culture

Teachers can become sensitized to the social and cultural context of childhood through reading such books as O. W. Richie and M. R. Koller, **Sociology of Childhood** (Appleton, 1963) and J. H. S. Bossard and E. S. Boll, **Sociology of Child Development** (Harper & Row, 1966). These treatments view the child, primarily, as a person being intro-

---

Everett T. Keach, Jr. is Professor, Social Science Education Department, College of Education, University of Georgia, Athens, Georgia.

duced to and acting within social systems. E. W. King and A. Kerber, **The Sociology of Early Childhood Education** (Van Nostrand Reinhold, 1968), focus upon the process and structure of socialization as it is manifested in curriculum development.

For the general reader, a lucid comprehensive interpretation of the child's development from birth to the age of five is treated in M. Beadle, **A Child's Mind** (Doubleday, 1970). This book helps to summarize the conclusions to be drawn from the more current research in child development. E. A. Frommer, **Voyage Through Childhood Into the Adult World** (Pergamon, 1969, pb), also for nonprofessionals, presents an account of child development in terms of parent-child communication, temperament, and levels of consciousness. E. Kawin, **Early and Middle Childhood** (Purdue, 1963, pb) offers an easy introduction to child culture through an examination of the physical, mental, and social-emotional characteristics of children during childhood.

F. J. Estvan and E. W. Estvan in **Child's World: His Social Perception** (Putnam, 1959) present an analysis and a theory of social perception during childhood. The reader is oriented to the nature of social perception and the factors associated with its development among first- and sixth-grade children. In a similar vein, Dorothy Flapan, **Children's Understanding of Social Interaction** (Columbia Teachers College, 1968, pb) is useful in noting developmental trends in the child's ability to describe and make inferences about aspects of interpersonal relationships. A comparison of the cultural contexts of childhood can be found in Urie Bronfenbrenner, **Two Worlds of Childhood: US and USSR** (Russell Sage, 1970). Translated from the Russian language, K. Chukovsky's **From Two to Five** (Univ. of California, 1963, pb) describes the development of language and thought processes of the young child.

For the Serious Student

M. E. Breckenridge and M. N. Murphy, **Growth and Development of the Young Child** (Saunders, 1963), present a comprehensive view of the development of the child up to the age of five. Of special interest are the discussions of family influences and the development of concepts of self and others. Another useful reading is L. J. Stone and J. Church, **Childhood and Adolescence: A Psychology of the Growing Person** (Random House, 1968). Scholarly and readable chapters focusing upon the infant and preschool child are included with those of early childhood. P. H. Mussen, J. J. Conger, and J. Kagan, **Child Development and Personality** (Harper & Row, 1969, pb), also treat the same general range but with research references which are intended for the serious student. Another theoretical framework for studying the development of the child is offered by R. C. Johnson and G. Medinnus, **Child Psychology—Behavior and Development** (Wiley, 1969). C. Landreth, **Early**

Childhood: Behavior and Learning (Knopf, 1967) is highlighted by the chapters on language development and trends in the study of children's behaviors.

A strong influence in the work of those concerned with the cognitive development of the child is the work and writings of Jean Piaget. H. G. Furth, **Piaget for Teachers** (Prentice-Hall, 1970, pb) is intended for teachers with little background in Piagetian theory. With a background, the reader can learn more about Piaget's position on the development of logical thought processes during childhood from H. Ginsberg and S. Opper, **Piaget's Theory of Intellectual Development: An Introduction** (Prentice-Hall, 1969, pb). The presentation elaborates upon but does not oversimplify Piaget's theory. Jean Piaget and B. Inhelder, **Psychology of the Child** (Basic Books, 1969) serves as a summarization of his work in child psychology. The work is somewhat difficult to comprehend for those unfamiliar with Piagetian theory.

Child Culture: Implications for the Curriculum

J. Kagan, **Understanding Children** (Harcourt, 1971, pb) concentrates upon children's changing motivations and thought processes. The implications for teaching which are drawn from the theoretical essays are stated in clear and practical terms. M. Brearley, **Fundamentals in the First School** (Basil Blackwell, 1969) illustrates principles of child growth and development with curricular examples developed by a team of educators from the Froebel Institute College of Education in London. M. Brearley, **Teaching of Young Children** (Schocken Books, 1970) offers the reader an opportunity to examine the application of Piagetian Theory in selected British schools which have adapted to the "integrated day" concept. K. Read, **Nursery School** (Saunders, 1971) contains chapters on curriculum development and understanding human behavior which blend theory with particularly helpful applications. K. R. Baker and X. F. Fane, **Understanding and Guiding Young Children** (Prentice-Hall, 1970) contains comprehensive information on the child's physical, social, psychological and intellectual development. An easily read book on developmental behaviors and practical ways to work with the child in a family setting is found in D. V. Brown and P. McDonald, **Learning Begins at Home** (Lawrence, 1969, pb). Of interest to teachers is the book by J. Russell, **Creative Dance in the Primary School** (Praeger, 1968). Many ideas for individual curriculum applications are suggested which are based upon the observations of the child's life-space. N. McCashin, **Creative Dramatics in the Classroom** (David McKay, 1968) offers a rationale for creative dramatics which involves utilizing the child's play impulses to learn about himself and others.

Two journals are recommended for those seeking current references to research and trends in child growth and development. The general reader is referred to *Child Study* (Child Study Assn. of America, New York). For the serious student, *Child Development* (Society for Research in Child Development, Univ. of Chicago) is worthwhile reading. Brief reports on child development, cultural factors influencing children, and child rearing as reported to the Clearinghouse for Research in Child Life have been published in **Research Relating to Children: Bulletin No. 26** (HEW SRS, Children's Bureau, 1969). Since 1970, the ERIC Clearinghouse on Early Childhood Education has assumed the production of **Research Relating to Children.**

30

Adolescent Society

MAURICE P. HUNT

To understand adolescent society, social studies teachers may wish adolescents defined as persons and as students. They may be helped by reading critiques of social values and school practices which drive these students out of school. Finally, they may wish to know what the drop-outs believe and do, in order to understand their potential followers still in school. As more books are written by older adolescents and social commentators than by and about high school students, teachers will perforce select some books about the older groups which influence high school students.

What Is the Meaning of Adolescence?

Margaret Mead made us aware that adolescence is a cultural phenomenon; it is biological only to the extent that it is usually thought to begin with puberty. Our new cultural thinking holds that adolescence ends when a person finds a set of integrated values to carry him through life. Hence, the importance of recent books dealing with youth's achieving personhood – a condition of self-awareness, escape from alienation, achievement of a sense of purpose and identity. For definitions of adolescence according to this view see: Theodore Lidz, **The Person: His Development Throughout the Life Cycle** (Basic Books, 1968). Erik H. Erikson, **Identity: Youth and Crisis** (Norton, 1968) is original and impactful. Even though Erikson is perhaps naive on the political-

Maurice P. Hunt is Professor of Educational Foundations, Department of Secondary Education, College of Education, California State University, Fresno, California.

power matrix which makes self-identity hard to find, his analysis is valuable. Paul Goodman's classic **Growing Up Absurd** (Random House, 1960, pb) shows how cultural contradictions make self-identity difficult to achieve. Edgar Z. Friedenberg, **The Vanishing Adolescent** (Beacon, 1959, Dell, pb) examines the impact of the continuous shortening of time available for a young person to find himself.

How Does Our Culture Drive Adolescents from School?

With United States culture in a state of advanced disorganization, our present cultural crisis makes even the best schooling seem irrelevant to many teenagers. Paul Lauter and Florence Howe in **The Conspiracy of the Young** (World, 1970), a penetrating analysis of the culture, conclude that there is a war of values between young and old and that a genuine counter-culture exists into which teenage youth are being drawn from school. Kenneth Keniston's **The Uncommitted: Alienated Youth in American Society** (Harcourt, 1965, Dell, pb) contains good material on adolescence and varieties of alienation. Warren G. Bennis and Philip E. Slater in **The Temporary Society** (Harper & Row, 1968, pb) show how rapid change destroys traditional social controls and frees youth to seek a new out-of-school culture pattern. In **Culture and Commitment: A Study of the Generation Gap** (Doubleday, 1970) Margaret Mead shows how the central problem of youth today is finding values worth committing oneself to. Not finding them in school, teenagers drop out. Even more reasons for rebellion against school are cited by Jules Henry in **Culture Against Man** (Random House, 1963, pb), one of the most respected analyses of American culture. A puzzler for many persons is the large number of drop-outs among affluent youth. One concise answer is given (particularly pp. 308-309) in Alexander Klein, ed., **Natural Enemies??? Youth and the Clash of Generations** (Lippincott, 1969).

Adult leftists have achieved much admiration from youth and weakened their attachment to traditional middle-class schools. An example is seen in Marion K. Sanders, **The Professional Radical: Conversations with Saul Alinsky** (Harper & Row, 1970, pb). For a first-rate bibliography on how poverty drives students from school, see Bernard Goldstein, **Low Income Youth in Urban Areas: A Critical Review of the Literature** (Holt, Rinehart and Winston, 1967, pb).

Damned by most reviewers as simplistic, however one views Charles A. Reich's best selling **The Greening of America** (Random House, 1970, Bantam, pb) it is an attempt at provocative cultural analysis which provides valuable clues about youthful rebellion. Readers of Reich may want to read also Philip Nobile, **The Con III Controversy: The Critics Look at the Greening of America** (Simon & Shuster, 1971, pb).

A debated but carefully reasoned and factually grounded book is Theodore Roszak's **The Making of a Counter Culture** (Doubleday, 1969, pb). Roszak's book is considered by many to be one of the best analyses available on the dilemmas and future roles of youth in our culture. Robert D. Barr, ed., **Values and Youth** (NCSS, 1971, pb) is a booklet of some original and some reprinted readings that state and comment on many teenagers' views and feelings.

How Do Specific School Policies and Acts Drive Students Away?

Both students and critics of the schools complain steadily that the curriculum of most schools is obsolete — out of touch with the students' real world. "Why waste time with it?" many youth ask. In answer, Jerome S. Bruner, **The Relevance of Education** (Norton, 1971) recommends a revolutionary overhaul. Perhaps the best book of readings on the subject is William Van Til's **Curriculum: Quest for Relevance** (Houghton Mifflin, 1971). Administration policy is often behind the drop-out problem. For a well-documented criticism of how school administrators are educated and selected, see Raymond E. Callahan, **Education and the Cult of Efficiency: A Study of the Social Forces That Have Shaped the Administration of the Public Schools** (Univ. of Chicago, 1962, pb). Case studies appear in Solomon O. Lichter, **The Drop-Outs: A Treatment Study of Intellectually Capable Students Who Drop Out of High School** (Free Press, 1962, pb).

A highly provocative book on high-school inadequacies is Edgar Z. Friedenberg, **Coming of Age in America** (Random House, 1965, pb). Friedenberg argues that on behalf of institutional conveniences, students are denied autonomy, personal desires, and even intellectual creativity. Most reviewers think today's best writer on students hating high school and leaving it is Charles E. Silberman. His **Crisis in the Classroom: The Remaking of American Education** (Random House, 1970, pb) is jammed with solid support for his thesis that our schools are "mindless." His **Crisis in Black and White** (Random House, 1964, pb) is regarded as the best book on race relations in school.

One of our sharpest critics of conventional education is John Holt in his **How Children Fail, How Children Learn, The Under-Achieving School** (Pitman, 1964, 1967, 1969, pb), and **What Do I Do on Monday?** (Dutton, 1970). Some critics think Holt a little shallow and unduly in the tradition of Rousseau's Romantic Naturalism; but he is worth reading. Neil Postman and Charles Weingartner have two very interesting volumes: **Teaching as a Subversive Activity** (Delacorte, 1969), in which they argue that unless students are encouraged to raise touchy questions, school is a waste of time; and **The Soft Revolution: A Student Handbook for Turning Schools Around** (Delacorte, 1969, 1971). The latter is studded with imaginative and amusing student ploys to make teachers and principals so nervous they will reorganize school practice in self-defense. Peter Schrag, **Voices in the Classroom: Public Schools and Public Attitudes** (Beacon, 1965, pb) seems to have anticipated somewhat Postman and Weingartner. His hero is the nonconformist teacher who has nerve to ask the right questions, come what may. Patricia Sexton, ed., **School Policy and Issues in a Changing Society** (Allyn & Bacon, 1971) contains a number of readings by familiar names and some on outdated subjects, but also enough fresh reading to be worthwhile. Paul Goodman's **Compulsory Mis-Education** (Horizon, 1964, Random, pb) is a shatteringly angry criticism of the entire range of schooling in America from one of our most forceful critics.

What Do Teenagers Do When They Drop Out?

Establishment readers searching a common language ground with youth will find indispensable Eugene E. Landy's **The Underground Dictionary** (Simon & Shuster, 1971). You cannot understand the players without this program — either face to face or in the literature. With this dictionary, readers will better understand writing of both youth and their social critics. Marc Libarle and Tom Seligson, eds., **The High School Revolutionaries** (Vintage, 1970, pb) includes the hyper-intellectual writing of an 11th-grade drop-out, a Skinnerian future-planner. Ethel Grodzins Romm's **The Open Conspiracy** (Avon, 1971, pb) contains excerpts from street-corner publications plus Romm's analysis of both the drop-out drug culture and the political movement's broad spectrum from nihilists to do-gooders. Michael Brown's **The Politics and Anti-Politics of the Young** (Glencoe, 1969, pb) also covers both activists searching answers to America's problems and, very clearly, the disengaged hippies retired into their own life style. These two discerning books can be recommended as must reading for understanding current youth activities and beliefs. Additional information on new homes-away-from-home will be found in Roy Ald's **The Youth Communes: An Articulate Analysis of the Movement of American Youth Toward Communal Living** (Tower, 1970, pb). Based on a limited sample, it does not present a portrait of a heavenly life, but it does contain some most interesting commentary.

Several magazines are also useful. One is a quarterly, *Adolescence,* ed. William Kroll (Libra); another, for young adolescents, is *Junior Statesman,* ed. Kathy Newman (Junior Statesman). Older adolescents will be interested in *Teenville,* ed. Bob Fischer (Celebrity Publications); *Youth and Society,* ed. A. W. McEachern (Sage); and *Youth Service News,* ed. Milton J. Beniot (New York State Division of Youth).

31

Young Adults and Continuing Education

EUGENE I. JOHNSON

Adult or continuing education has become central to the continued progress of American society. It is a major resource in the enrichment and development of the lives of millions of Americans. Yet it remains in a peripheral position with respect to most of the formal institutions of education in this country. For that reason, it is difficult to develop a complete picture of the range of persons who participate in continuing education, their reasons for doing so, the institutional sponsorship under which they enroll, and the almost endless variety of methods employed. All of the fissures in the mosaic of continuing education are reflected in miniature when the focus is narrowed to the young adult who, for purposes of this report, are considered to be (a) not in the regular secondary system and (b) in age somewhere between 17 and 35. The U.S. Census Bureau classifies basic information about the educational pursuits of young people in the 17-24 and 25-35 age brackets in continuing education as: (1) statistical reports on the number engaged in both part-time and full-time educational activity; (2) the several different subcultures that exist within the general stream of *young adults* and which represent distinct targets for different kinds of educational programs; and (3) the institutional or organizational auspices for continuing education: military force, colleges and universities, correctional institutions, public schools, and others. The books included in this brief survey have been grouped in those three categories.

Eugene I. Johnson is Professor of Adult Education, College of Education, University of Georgia, Athens, Georgia.

Which Young Adults Participate in Continuing Education?

Several studies made over the past decade present what evidence there is regarding the continuing education of young people who have left the regular school system. The most comprehensive of these, although based on population sample studies in only a small number of cities, was conducted by the National Opinion Research Center and reported by Ralph W. Johnstone and Ramon Rivera in **Volunteers for Learning** (Aldine, 1965). Section IV considers young adults. At the end of the decade, Imogene E. Okes reported in **Participation in Adult Education** (USGPO, 1971) that a higher percentage of young adults participated in continuing education than the entire population over age 17; that more men than women enrolled in courses; and that participation was related to such significant variables as level of previous education completed, race and occupation. A. A. Liveright's **Study of Adult Education in the United States** (Center for the Study of the Liberal Education of Adults, 1966) agrees generally with the other studies, but focuses on the social, economic and technological trends that produce the need for and shape offerings in continuing education along with the pattern of institutional support and resources. **The Young Voter: A Guide to Instruction About Voter Behavior and Elections** (NCSS, 1972), by John J. Patrick and Allen D. Glenn, will also be valuable for teachers.

Who Are the Young Adults?

The young adults bridge the years between adolescence and the mid-thirties when middle-class success in jobs, stability in family life, and the acceptance of responsibilty in community and national decision-making have been achieved. There are distinctive subcultures in young adult society, particularly since various subcultures are the target of extensive efforts to involve their members in educational programs, both formal and informal. The subcultures are often intimately related to the aspirations of racial and other minority groups in the country and to the problem of poverty. Often the subcultures reflect both poverty and minority issues. Accounts of educational programs addressed to young adult gangs, or to poor people in rural areas, are found generally at the present time only in official reports to sponsoring agencies, occasional papers, or articles in professional journals. Of the few studies readily available, Barbara H. Kemp's **Youth We Haven't Served** and **Training the Hard Core Unemployed,** the report of a demonstration-research project at Virginia State College in Norfolk (USGPO, 1966, 1964, pb), discuss needs of school drop-outs and other deprived young people and their programs. Martin W. Essex, **Human Impact of Adult Basic Education** (Ohio State Dept. of Educ., 1970) presents the value of such programs through the eyes of participants. Most reports of education on disadvantaged young adults have not yet generally passed through the eye and out of the pen of the professional writer.

However, useful accounts of the culture of these groups do exist. Paul Hirsch in **The Young Toughs** (Pyramid, 1970, pb) and Alan Bestic in **Turn Me On, Man** (Award, 1966, pb) present vivid portraits of some of the many gangs that exist in the young adult group. Other publications seek to relate or explain the civic violence that characterized many cities in the 1960's in terms of the lack of relevance of education to the aspirations and frustrations of young adults caught in the trap of urban poverty, overlaid usually with racial discrimination. Excellent, although terrifying examples of this, are R. E. Conot's **Rivers of Blood, Years of Darkness** (Bantam, 1968, pb) describing the Watts area of Los Angeles; Sterling Tucker's **Beyond the Burning** (Assn., 1968, pb) about the events in Washington, D.C., following the assassination of Martin Luther King; and Kenneth B. Clark's **Dark Ghetto** (Harper & Row, 1965, pb).

Young adults who have become the target of extensive efforts for educational programs in poverty-riddled rural areas may be seen in such moving studies as Harry Caudill's **Night Comes to the Cumberland** (Atlantic Monthly, 1963, pb), W. D. Weatherford and E. D. C. Brewer's **Life and Religion in Southern Appalachia** (Friendship, 1962), and Paul Good's **The American Serfs** (Ballantine, 1968, pb).

Several books that relate information about life styles of subculture to the process of continuing education are Curtis Ulmer's **Teaching the Disadvantaged Adult** (NEA, 1969, pb), Edmonia Davidson's **Family and Personal Development in Adult Basic Education** (Natl. Univ. Extension Assn., 1971), and the volume of essays edited by Lola M. Ireland under the title **Low-Income Life Styles** (USGPO, 1967). It should be noted that many writers do not believe the disadvantaged person differs greatly from other segments of society in terms of values, aspirations, and reasons for participating in education on many social issues. For some discussion of this issue, see Frank Riessman's **The Culturally Deprived Child** (Harper & Row, 1962) and the report by B. O. Smith, Cohen and Pearl, prepared for the Institute for Advanced Study in Teaching Disadvantaged Youth, entitled **Teachers for the Real World** (American Assn. of Colleges for Teacher Education, 1969).

Young Adults and Institutional Programs of Continuing Education

Institutions or organizations that include large numbers of young adults are the public schools, colleges and universities (including community colleges), business and industry, military forces, churches, correctional institutions, and a dozen other major categories. Separate studies of the young adults in these programs may be found in several recent major publications. **The Handbook of Adult Education in the**

United States (Adult Education Assn., 1970) describes twelve different institutional programs. N. B. Shaw, ed., **Administration of Continuing Education** (NEA, 1970) presents several authors with comments about the nature of the adult participant and the educational issues raised by attempts to develop more effective programs. James T. Carey's **Forms and Forces in University Adult Education** (Center for the Study of the Liberal Education of Adults, 1961) provides both statistical information and developing trends among young adults who become part-time students in universities or colleges. Generally speaking, the young adult who is not a full-time college student does not associate closely with full-time students and his values tend to reflect the larger society than that of campus youth. For black students, however, the barriers between him and higher education lead him to identify with militant blacks in the general effort, of which education is only one factor, to open the doors to full and equal participation by blacks in American society. For an account of the problems black young adults face in continuing their education, see Fred E. Crossland's **Minority Access to College,** prepared for the Ford Foundation (Schocken, 1971).

About half of the nation's high school graduates now enter college. By age 20 a considerably large proportion have completed junior college or dropped out in favor of full-time employment. Teachers and other educators tend, of course, to give their major attention to those enrolled or otherwise involved in schooling, But the cold, raw statistics clearly reveal that, while many in various ways may be acting and continuing in education, a majority discontinue regular, official schooling no later than the average age of about 17. By the age of 20 only a small proportion of youths are school participants. The several references recommended for your consideration can be useful in recognizing the educational implications of this fact.

Directory of Publishers

Abbey House, 8 Victoria St., London, S.W. England

Academic Press, Inc., 111 Fifth Ave., New York, N. Y. 10003

Addison-Wesley Publishing Co., Inc., Reading, Mass. 01867

Adler's Foreign Books, Inc., 162 Fifth Ave., New York, N. Y. 10010

Adult Education Association of the USA, 810 18th St., N.W., Washington, D. C. 20006

Aldine-Atherton, Inc., 529 S. Wabash Ave., Chicago, Ill. 60605

Allyn & Bacon, Inc., 470 Atlantic Ave., Boston, Mass. 02210

American Academy of Arts & Sciences, 7 Linden St., Cambridge, Mass. 02138

American Academy of Political & Social Science (AAPSS), 3937 Chestnut St., Philadelphia, Pa. 19104

American Anthropological Assn., 1703 New Hampshire Ave., N.W., Washington, D. C. 20009

American Association for the Advancement of Science, 1515 Mass. Ave., N.W., Washington, D. C. 20005

American Association for Health, Physical Education and Recreation, 1201 16th St., N.W., Washington, D. C. 20036

American Association of Colleges for Teacher Education, 1201 16th St., N.W., Washington, D. C. 20036

American Book Company, 450 W. 33rd St., New York, N. Y. 10001

American Council on Education, One Dupont Circle, N.W., Washington, D. C. 20036

American Education Publications, 245 Long Hill Rd., Middletown, Conn. 06457

American Elsevier Publishing Co., 52 Vanderbilt Ave., New York, N. Y. 10017

American Heritage Press (See McGraw-Hill Book Co.)

American Historical Association, 400 A St., S.E., Washington, D. C. 20003

American Library Association, 50 E. Huron St., Chicago, Ill. 60611

American Newspaper Publishers Association, 750 Third Ave., New York, N. Y. 10017

American Psychological Association, 1200 17th St., N.W., Washington, D. C. 20036

American Scholar, 1811 Q St., N.W., Washington, D. C. 20009

American School Health Association, 1740 Broadway, Fifteenth Floor, New York, N. Y. 10019

American Sociological Association, 1722 N St., N.W., Washington, D. C. 20036

Amphoto, 915 Broadway, New York, N. Y. 10010

Anchor (See Doubleday & Co.)

Anchor Enterprises, Box 1656, Manhattan Beach, Calif. 90266

Annual Reviews Inc., 4159 El Camino Way, Palo Alto, Calif. 94306

Appleton-Century-Crofts, 440 Park Ave., S., New York, N. Y. 10016

Association of American Geographers, 1710 16th St., N.W., Washington, D. C. 20009

Association Press, 291 Broadway, New York, N. Y. 10008

Atheneum Publishers, 122 E. 42nd St., New York, N. Y. 10017

Atherton Press, Inc. (See Aldine-Atherton, Inc.)

Atlantic Monthly Press, 8 Arlington St., Boston, Mass. 02116

Avon Books, 959 Eighth Ave., New York, N. Y. 10019

Award Books, 235 E. 45th St., New York, N. Y. 10017

Ballantine Books, Inc., 101 Fifth Ave., New York, N. Y. 10003

Bantam Books, Inc., 666 Fifth Ave., New York, N. Y. 10019

Barnes & Noble Books (See Harper & Row)

Barre Publishers, South St., Barre, Mass. 01005

Basic Books, Inc., Publishers, 10 E. 53rd St., New York, N. Y. 10022

Beacon Press, Inc., 25 Beacon St., Boston, Mass. 02108

Bedminster Press, Vreeland Ave., Totowa, N. J. 07512

Behavioral Research Laboratories, Ladera Professional Center, Box 577, Palo Alto, Calif. 94302

Benziger Brothers, Inc., 866 Third Ave., New York, N. Y. 10022

Basil Blackwell, 108 Cowley Rd., Oxford, OX41JF, England

Blaisdell, Xerox College Publications, 275 Wyman St., Waltham, Mass. 02154

Bobbs-Merrill Company, 4300 W. 62nd St., Indianapolis, Ind. 46268

R. R. Bowker Co., 1180 Ave. of the Americas, New York, N. Y. 10036

George Braziller, Inc., 1 Park Ave., New York, N. Y. 10016

Brookings Institution, 1775 Mass. Ave., N.W., Washington, D. C. 20036

Brooklyn College (CUNY), City University of New York, Brooklyn, N. Y. 11210

Brooks/Cole Publishing Co., 540 Abrego St., Monterey, Calif. 93940

Brown Book Co., 519 Acorn St. Deer Park, N. Y. 11729

Burgess Publishing Co., 426 S. Sixth St., Minneapolis, Minn. 55415

Cambridge Book Co., 488 Madison Ave., New York, N. Y. 10022

Cambridge University Press, 32 E. 57th St., New York, N. Y. 10022

Canfield Press, 850 Montgomery St., San Francisco, Calif. 94133

Capricorn Books, 200 Madison Ave., New York, N. Y. 10016

Celebrity Service, Inc., 171 W. 57th St., New York, N. Y. 10019

Center for Applied Research in Education, 70 Fifth Ave., New York, N. Y. 10011

Center for Study of Liberal Education for Adults (CSLEA), Syracuse University, 105 Roney Lane, Syracuse, N. Y. 13210

Central Atlantic Regional Ed. Lab., Washington, D. C.

Central Midwestern Regional Educational Laboratory (CMREL), 10646 St. Charles Rock Rd., St. Ann, Mo. 63074

C. Chandler Co., Newcastle, New Hampshire 03854

Child Study Association of America, 9 E. 89th St., New York, N. Y. 10028

Chilton Book Company, 401 Walnut St., Philadelphia, Pa. 19106

Citation Press (See Scholastic Magazines, Inc.)

Clarendon Press, Clarendon, Tex. 79226

Collier Books (See Crowell Collier & Macmillan)

Columbia University Press, 562 W. 113th St., New York 10025

Committee for Economic Development, 477 Madison Ave., New York, N. Y. 10022

Cornell University Press, 124 Robert Pl., Ithaca, N. Y. 14850

Council in Spanish American Work, 120 W. 44th St., New York, N. Y. 10036

Coward-McCann, Inc., 200 Madison Ave., New York, N. Y. 10016

Creative Educational Society, 515 N. Front St., Mankato, Minn. 56001

Criterion Books, 257 Park Ave., S., New York, N. Y. 10010

Cromwell Textbooks, 734 Brompton Ave., Chicago, Ill. 60657

Crowell Collier & Macmillan, 866 Third Ave., New York, N. Y. 10022

Thomas Y. Crowell Co., 666 Fifth Ave., New York, N. Y. 10019

Crown Publishers, 419 Park Ave., S., New York, N. Y. 10016

David-Stewart Publishing Co., 5257 N. Dacoma Ave., Indianapolis, Ind. 46220

John Day Co., 257 Park Ave., S., New York, N. Y. 10010

Delacorte Press (See Dell Publishing Co., Inc.)

Dell Publishing Co., Inc., 750 Third Ave., New York, N. Y. 10017

Dembar Educational Research Services, Box 1605, Madison, Wisc. 53701

Dial Press (See Dell Publishing Co., Inc.)

Dimension Books, Inc., Box 811, Denville, N. J. 07834

Dodd, Mead & Co., 79 Madison Ave., New York, N. Y. 10016

Dorsey Press (See Richard D. Irwin, Inc.)

Doubleday & Co., Inc., 501 Franklin Ave., Garden City, N. Y. 11530

Dow Jones Books, Box 300, Princeton, N. J. 08540

E. P. Dutton & Co., Inc., 201 Park Ave., S., New York, N. Y. 10003

Education Commission of the States, 1860 Lincoln St., Denver, Colo. 80203

Educational Resource Information Center (ERIC-ChESS), 855 Broadway, Boulder, Colo. 80302

Educational Testing Service, 20 Nassau St., Princeton, N. J. 08540

Educators Progress Service, Box 497, Randolph, Wisc. 53956

Encyclopedia Brittannica Educational Corp., 425 N. Michigan Ave., Chicago, Ill. 60611

Everett-Edwards, Inc., 133 S. Pecan, DeLand, Fla. 32720

Farrar, Straus & Giroux, Inc., 19 Union Sq. W., New York, N. Y. 10003

Fearon Publishers, 6 Davis Dr., Belmont, Calif. 94002

J. G. Ferguson Publishing Co., 6 N. Michigan Ave., Chicago, Ill. 60602

Field Educational Publications, 2400 Hanover St., Palo Alto., Calif. 94304

Fleet Press Corp., 156 Fifth Ave., New York, N. Y. 10010

Foreign Policy Assn., 345 E. 46th St., New York, N. Y. 10017

Fortress Press, 2900 Queen Lane, Philadelphia, Pa. 19129

Foundation Press, 170 Old Country Rd., Mineola, N.Y. 11501

Foundation Publishers, 4101 San Jacinto St., Houston Tex. 10022

Free Press (See Macmillan Co.)

W. H. Freeman & Co., 660 Market St., San Francisco, Calif. 94104

Freeman, Cooper & Co., 1736 Stockton St., San Francisco, Calif. 94133

Friends of the Earth, 101 Fifth Ave., New York, N.Y. 10003

Friendship Press, 475 Riverside Dr., New York, N.Y. 10027

General Welfare Publications, Box 19098, Sacramento, Calif. 95819

Ginn and Co., 191 Spring St., Lexington, Mass. 02173

Glencoe Press, 866 Third Ave., New York, N.Y. 10022

Golden Press, 1220 Mound Ave., Racine, Wisc. 53404

Goodyear Publishing Co., Inc. (See Prentice-Hall)

Greenwood Publishing Corp., 51 Riverside Ave., Westport, Conn. 06880

Grosset & Dunlap., 51 Madison Ave., New York, N.Y. 10010

Grossman Publishers, (See Viking Press, Inc.)

Grove Press, 53 E. 11th St., New York, N.Y. 10003

Gryphon Press, 220 Montgomery St., Highland Park, N. J. 08904

Guidance Associates, 41 Washington Ave., Pleasantville, N. Y. 10570

Hammond Inc., Maplewood, N.J. 07040

Harcourt Brace Jovanovich, Inc., 757 Third Ave., New York, N. Y. 10017

Harper & Row Publishers, 10 E. 53rd St. New York, N. Y. 10022

Harvard University Press, Kittridge Hall, 79 Garden St., Cambridge, Mass. 02138

Hawthorn Books, 70 Fifth Ave., New York, N. Y. 10011

Dept. of Health, Education and Welfare, 400 Maryland Ave., S. W., Washington, D. C. 20202

D. C. Heath Co., 125 Spring St., Lexington, Mass. 02173

James H. Heineman, Inc., Publishers, 475 Park Ave, New York, N. Y. 10022

Hill & Wang, Inc. (See Farrar, Straus & Giroux Inc.)

Hogarth Press, Box 6012, Honolulu, Hawaii 96818

Holbrook Press, (See Allyn & Bacon, Inc.)

Holt, Rinehart & Winston Inc., 383 Madison Ave., New York, N. Y. 10017

Horizon Press, 156 Fifth Ave., New York, N. Y. 10010

Houghton Mifflin Co., 110 Tremont St., Boston, Mass. 02107

Humanities Press, Inc., 303 Park Ave., S., New York, N.Y. 10010

Images Press, 2264 Green St., San Francisco, Calif. 94123

Indian Historian, Box 1964, Santa Fe, N. M. 87501

Indiana University Press, Tenth & Morton Sts., Bloomington, Ind. 47401

International Publishers Co., Inc., 381 Park Ave, S., New York, N. Y. 10017

Interstate Printers and Publishers, Inc., 19 North Jackson St., Danville, Ill. 61832

Intext Educational Publishers, Oak St. & Pawnee Ave., Scranton, Pa. 18515

Iowa State University Press, Press Bldg., Ames, Iowa 50010

Richard D. Irwin, Inc., 1818 Ridge Rd., Homewood, Ill. 60430

Johnson Reprint Corp. (See Academic Press)

Joint Council on Economic Education, 1212 Ave. of the Americas, New York, N. Y. 10036

Marshall Jones Co., Francestown, N.H. 03043

Jossey-Bass, Inc., Publishers, 615 Montgomery St., San Francisco, Calif. 94111

Junior Statesman Foundation, 495 California Ave., Palo Alto, Calif. 94306

Knopf, Alfred A., (See Random House)

Norman Lathrop, Enterprises, Box 83, Flint, Mich. 48501

Lawrence Publishing Co., 617 S. Olive St., Los Angeles, Calif. 90014

Lawyers Cooperative Publishing Co., Aqueduct Bldg., Rochester, N.Y. 14603

Learning Systems Co., (See Richard D. Irwin, Inc.)

Libra Publishers, Box 165, 391 Willets Rd., Roslyn Heights, N.Y. 11577

Lincoln Filene Center, Tufts University Medford, Mass. 02155

J. B. Lippincott Co., E. Washington Sq., Philadelphia, Pa. 19105

Little, Brown & Co., 34 Beacon St., Boston, Mass. 02106

Littlefield, Adams & Co., 81 Adams Dr., Totowa, N.J. 17512

Longman, Green & Co., 750 Third Ave., New York, N.Y. 10017

Lothrop, Lee & Shepard Co., (See William Morrow & Co., Inc.)

McCutchan Publishing Corp., 2526 Grove St., Berkeley, Calif. 94704

McClelland & Stewart, 25 Hollinger Rd., Toronto 16, Canada

McGraw-Hill Book Co., 1221 Ave. of the Americas, New York, N.Y. 10020

David McKay Co., Inc., 750 Third Ave., New York, N.Y. 10017

McKinley Publishing Co., 112 S. New Broadway, Brooklawn, N.J. 08030

Macmillan Company, 866 Third Ave., New York, N.Y. 10022

Macrae Smith Co., 225 S. 15th St., Philadelphia, Pa. 19102

Marin County Public Schools, Corte Madera, Calif. 94925

Markham Publishing Co., 3322 W. Peterson Ave., Chicago, Ill. 60659

Mentor Press, 150 Fifth Ave., New York, N.Y. 10011

Meredith Press, 70 Fifth Ave., New York, N.Y. 10011

Meridian Books, (See World Pub. Co.)

Charles E. Merrill, Publishing Co., 1300 Alum Creek Dr., Columbus, Ohio 43216

Julian Messner, 1 W. 39th St., New York, N.Y. 10018

Methuen, 105 Fifth Ave., New York, N.Y. 10003

Michigan State University Press, Box 550, East Lansing, Mich. 48823

Modern Library, (See Random House)

William Morrow & Co., 105 Madison Ave., New York, N.Y. 10016

National Assn. of Broadcasters, 1771 N St., N.W., Washington, D.C. 20036

National Assn. of Educational Broadcasters, 1346 Connecticut Ave., N. W., Washington, D.C. 20036

National Assn. of Mental Health, 10 Columbus Circle, Suite 1300, New York, N.Y. 10019

National Audubon Society, 1130 Fifth Ave., New York, N.Y. 10028

National Council for Geographic Education, 115 N. Marion Street, Oak Park, Ill. 60301

National Council for the Social Studies, 1201 16th St., N.W., Washington, D.C. 20036

National Education Association, 1201 16th St., N.W., Washington, D.C. 20036

National Foundation for Environmental Control, 151 Tremont St., Boston, Mass. 02111

National Institute of Mental Health, 5600 Fisher's Lane, Rockville, Md. 20852

National Press Books, 850 Hansen Way, Palo Alto, Calif. 94304

National School Public Relations Association, 1201 16th St., N.W., Washington, D.C. 20036

National University Extension Assn., 900 Silver Spring Ave., Silver Spring, Md. 20910

Natural History Press, (See Doubleday & Co.)

New American Library, 1301 Ave. of the Americas, New York, N.Y. 10019

New York Graphic Society, Ltd., 140 Greenwich Ave., Greenwich, Conn. 06830

New York State Division of Youth, Albany, N.Y. 12203

New York State Education Dept., 131 Livingston St., Brooklyn, N.Y. 11201

New York Times, 330 Madison Ave., New York, N.Y. 10017

New York University Press, Washington Square, New York, N.Y. 10003

North Carolina State Department of Public Instruction, Education Bldg., Raleigh, N.C. 27602

W. W. Norton & Co., 55 Fifth Ave., New York, N.Y. 10003

Oceana Publications, Inc., Dobbs-Ferry, N.Y. 10522

Ohio State Department of Education, Ohio Departments Building, Columbus, Ohio 43215

Ohio State University Press, 2070 Neil Ave., Columbus, Ohio 43210

Oxford University Press, Inc., 200 Madison Ave., New York, N.Y. 10016

Pantheon Books, Inc., (See Random House)

Parents Magazine Press, 52 Vanderbilt Ave., New York, N.Y. 10017

Peacock Press, Box 12142, Oakland, Calif. 94604

Pegasus, (See Bobbs-Merrill Co.)

Pelican Publishing House, 630 Burmaster St., Gretna, La. 70053

Penguin Books, Inc., 7110 Ambassador Rd., Baltimore, Md. 21207

Pergamon Press, Maxwell House, Fairview Park, Elmsford, N.Y. 10523

Phi Delta Kappan, 8th St. and Union Ave., Box 789, Bloomington, Ind. 47401

Philosophical Library, Inc., 15 E. 40th St., New York, N.Y. 10016

Pitman Publishing Corp., 6 East 43rd St., New York, N.Y. 10017

Pocket Books, (See Simon & Schuster)

Praeger Publishers, 111 Fourth Ave., New York, N.Y. 10003

Prentice-Hall, Inc., Englewood Cliffs, N.J. 07632

Princeton University Press, Princeton, N.J. 08540

Public Affairs Committee, 381 Park Ave. S., New York, N.Y. 10016

Public Affairs Press, 419 New Jersey Ave., S.E., Washington, D.C. 20003

Purdue University Studies, South Campus Courts, Purdue University, Lafayette, Ind. 47907

G. P. Putnam's Sons, 200 Madison Ave., New York, N.Y. 10016

Pyramid Press, 407 Industrial Park, Palm Springs, Calif. 92262

Quadrangle Books, (See New York Times)

Rand McNally & Co., 8255 Central Park Ave., Skokie, Ill. 60680

Random House, 201 E. 50th St., New York, N.Y. 10022

Reinhold Publishing Co., 450 W. 33rd St., New York, N.Y. 10001

Ronald Press Co., 79 Madison Ave., New York, N.Y. 10016

Royal University of Lund, Lund, Sweden

Rutgers University Press, 30 College Ave., New Brunswick, N.J. 08903

Russell Sage Foundation, 230 Park Ave., New York, N.Y. 10017

Sage Publications, Inc., 257 S. Beverly Dr., Beverly Hills, Calif. 90212

St. Martin's Press, Inc., 175 Fifth Ave., New York, N.Y. 10010

Saturday Review, 230 Park Ave., New York, N.Y. 10017

W. B. Saunders Co., 218 W. Washington Sq., Philadelphia, Pa. 19105

Schenkman Publishing Co., Inc., 3 Mt. Auburn Pl., Harvard Sq., Cambridge, Mass. 02138

Schocken Books, 200 Madison Ave., New York, N.Y. 10016

Scholastic Magazines, Inc., 50 W. 44th St., New York, N.Y. 10036

Science Research Associates (SRA), 259 E. Erie St., Chicago, Ill. 60611

Scott, Foresman & Co., 1900 E. Lake Ave., Glenview, Ill. 60025

Charles Scribner's Sons, 597 Fifth Ave., New York, N.Y. 10017

Signet Books, (See New American Library)

Simon and Schuster, Inc., 630 Fifth Ave., New York, N.Y. 10020

Social Science Education Consortium, 855 Broadway, Boulder, Colo. 80302

Society for Research in Child Development, 5801 Ellis Ave., Chicago, Ill. 60637

Southern Illinois University Press, McLafferty Rd., Box 697, Carbondale, Ill. 62901

Southwestern Co-op Educational Laboratory, 3456 International Blvd., Suite 221, Austin, Texas

South-Western Publishing Co., 5101 Madison Rd., Cincinnati, Ohio 45227

Spectrum Books, (See Prentice-Hall, Inc.)

Springer Publishing Co., Inc., 200 Park Ave., S., New York, N.Y. 10003

Stanford University Press, Stanford, Calif. 94107

Straight Arrow Books, 625 Third Ave., San Francisco, Calif. 94107

Syracuse University Press, Box 8, University Sta., Syracuse, N.Y. 13210

Tara Books, 56 Society St., Charleston, S.C. 29401

Teachers College Press, Columbia University, 1234 Amsterdam Ave., New York, N.Y. 10027

Torchbooks, Scranton, Pa. 18512

Tower Publications, 185 Madison Ave., New York, N.Y. 10016
Trimbelle Press, Prescott, Wisc. 54021
Tri-Ocean Books, 62 Townsend St., San Francisco, Calif. 94107
Tudor Publishing Co., 221 Park Ave., S., New York, N.Y. 10003
Twentieth Century Fund, 41 E. 70th St., New York, N.Y. 10021

UNESCO Publications Center, Box 433, UNIPUB, Inc., New York, N.Y. 10016
U.S. Chamber of Commerce, 1615 H St., N.W., Washington, D.C. 20006
U.S. Dept. of Commerce, National Bureau of Standards, Clearing House, Springfield, Va. 22151
U.S. Government Printing Office (GPO) Division of Public Documents, Washington, D.C. 20402
U.S. Office of Education (OE), 400 Maryland Ave., Washington, D.C. 20202
Universal Publishing and Distributing Corp., 235 E. 45th St., New York, N.Y. 10017
Universe Books, 381 Park Ave., S., New York, N.Y. 10016
University of California Press, 2223 Fulton St., Berkeley, Calif. 94720
University of Chicago Press, 5801 Ellis Ave., Chicago, Ill. 60637
University of Georgia Press, Waddel Hall, Athens, Ga. 30601
University of Illinois Press, Urbana, Ill. 61801
University of Michigan Press, 615 E. University, Ann Arbor, Mich. 48106
University of Minnesota Press, 2037 University Ave., S.E., Minneapolis, Minn.
University of New Mexico Press, Albuquerque, N.M. 87106
University of Notre Dame Press, Notre Dame, Ind. 46556
University of Tennessee Press, Communications Bldg., Knoxville, Tenn. 37916
University of Texas Press, Box 7819, University Station, Austin, Tex. 78712
University of Washington Press, Seattle Wash. 98105
University of Wisconsin Press, Box 1379, Madison, Wisc. 53701

Van Nostrand Reinhold Co., 459 W. 33rd St., New York, N.Y. 10001
Viking Press, Inc., 625 Madison Ave., New York, N.Y. 10022
Vintage College Books (See Random House)

Ward Waddell Jr., 495 San Fernando St., San Diego, Calif. 92106
Wadsworth Publishing Co., Belmont, Calif. 94002
West Publishing Co., 50 W. Kellogg Bend, St. Paul, Minn. 55102
West-Lewis Publishing Co., Box 1750, San Francisco, Calif. 94101
Westminster Press, Witherspoon Bldg., Philadelphia, Pa. 19107
John Wiley & Sons, Inc., 605 Third Ave., New York, N.Y. 10016
H. W. Wilson Co., 950 University Ave., Bronx, N.Y. 10452
World Law Fund, 11 W. 42nd St., New York, N.Y. 10036
World Publishing Co., 110 E. 59th St., New York, N.Y. 10022
World Trade Academy Press, 50 E. 42nd St., New York, N.Y. 10017

Xerox Education Group, 1200 High Ridge Rd., Stanford, Conn. 06905

Yale University Press, 92A Yale Station, New Haven, Conn. 06520

Index of Authors Cited in Chapters

1. THE SOCIAL SCIENCES

2. ANTHROPOLOGY

3. ECONOMICS

4. HUMAN GEOGRAPHY

5. UNITED STATES HISTORY

6. WORLD HISTORY

7. PSYCHOLOGY

8. POLITICAL SCIENCE

9. SOCIOLOGY

10. SOCIETAL PROBLEMS

11. CITIZENSHIP AND HUMAN RIGHTS

12. CURRENT EVENTS

13. SOCIAL FOUNDATIONS OF EDUCATION

14. ENVIRONMENTAL PROBLEMS AND CONSERVATION

15. HUMANITIES

16. INTERNATIONAL STUDIES

17. LAW AND JUSTICE

18. MASS COMMUNICATION IN SOCIETY

19. PHILOSOPHY AND SOCIAL VALUES

20. POPULATION AND URBANISM

21. SOCIAL PROBLEMS, SOCIAL PLANNING, AND CHANGE

22. POVERTY

23. PUBLIC HEALTH, ESPECIALLY DRUGS

24. INSTRUCTIONAL OBJECTIVES AND EVALUATION

25. GENERAL INSTRUCTION AND RESOURCES

26. ELEMENTARY SCHOOLS' TEACHING AND LEARNING

27. SECONDARY SCHOOLS' TEACHING AND LEARNING

28. GENERAL COLLEGES AND UNIVERSITIES

29. CHILD CULTURE

30. ADOLESCENT SOCIETY

31. YOUNG ADULTS AND CONTINUING EDUCATION

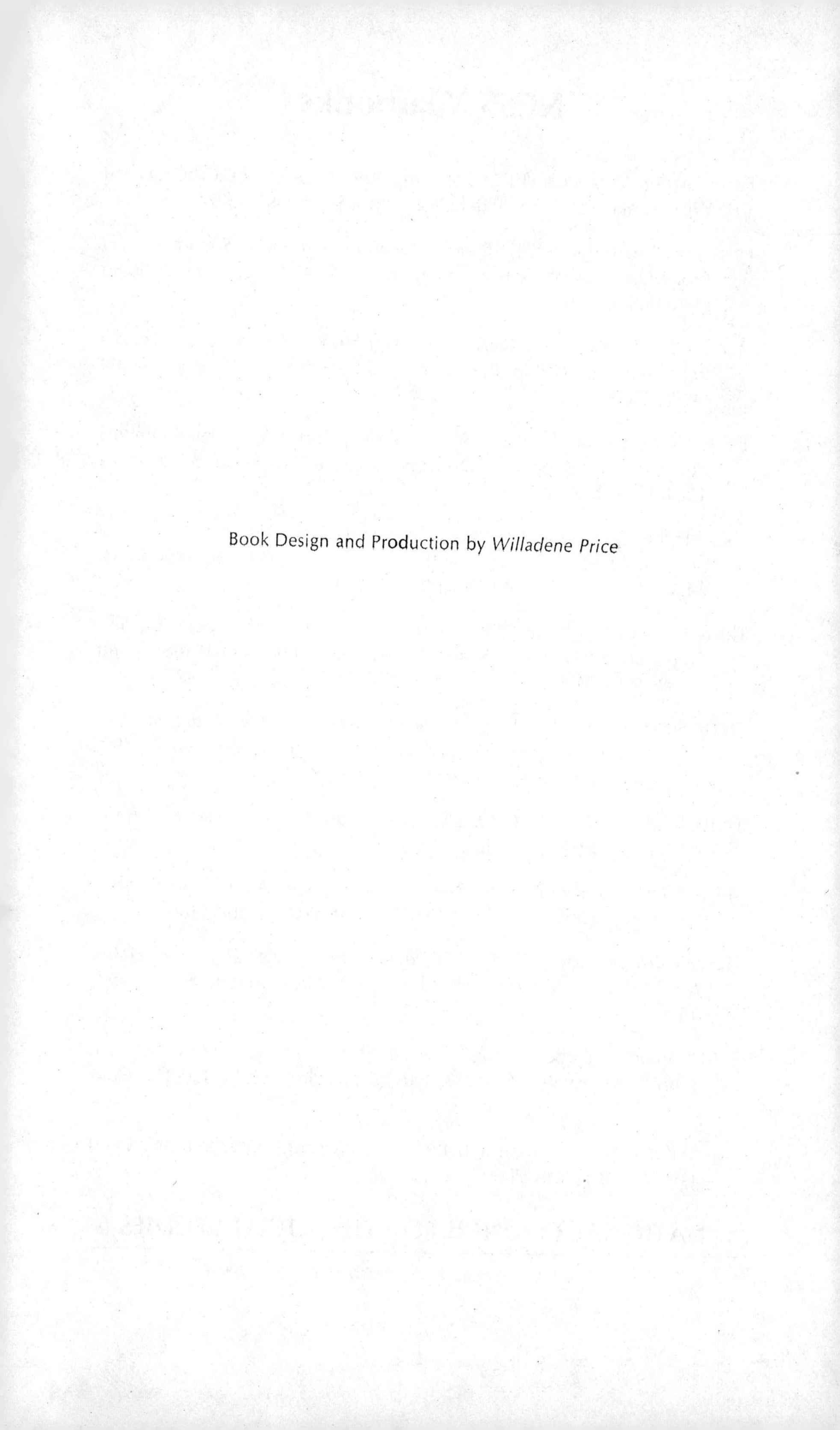

Book Design and Production by *Willadene Price*

NCSS Yearbooks

Forty-Second Yearbook (1972) *Teaching About Life in the City,* Richard Wisniewski, ed. $5.50 (490-15272); cloth $7.00 (490-15274).

Forty-First Yearbook (1971) *Values Education: Rationale, Strategies, and Procedures,* Lawrence E. Metcalf, ed. $5.00 (490-15268); cloth $6.50 (490-15270).

Fortieth Yearbook (1970) *Focus on Geography: Key Concepts and Teaching Strategies,* Phillip Bacon, ed. $5.50 (490-15264); cloth $7.00 (490-15266).

Thirty-Ninth Yearbook (1969) *Social Studies Curriculum Development: Prospects and Problems,* Dorothy McClure Fraser, ed. $4.50 (490-15240); cloth $5.50 (490-15242).

Thirty-Eighth Yearbook (1968) *International Dimensions in the Social Studies,* James M. Becker and Howard D. Mehlinger, co-editors. $4.50 (490-15212); cloth $5.50 (490-15214).

Thirty-Seventh Yearbook (1967) *Effective Thinking in the Social Studies,* Jean Fair and Fannie R. Shaftel, co-editors. $4.00 (490-15188); cloth $5.00 (490-15190).

Thirty-Sixth Yearbook (1966) *Political Science in the Social Studies,* Robert E. Cleary and Donald H. Riddle, co-editors. $4.00 (490-15162); cloth $5.00 (490-15160).

Thirty-Fifth Yearbook (1965) *Evaluation in Social Studies,* Harry D. Berg, ed. $4.00 (490-15128); cloth $5.00 (490-15126).

Thirty-Fourth Yearbook (1964) *New Perspectives in World History,* Shirley H. Engle, ed. $5.00 (490-15108); cloth $6.00 (490-15106).

Thirty-Third Yearbook (1963) *Skill Development in Social Studies,* Helen McCracken Carpenter, ed. $4.00 (490-15064); cloth $5.00 (490-15062).

Thirty-Second Yearbook (1962) *Social Studies in Elementary Schools,* John U. Michaelis, ed. $4.00 (490-15000); cloth $5.00 (490-14996).

Thirty-First Yearbook (1961) *Interpreting and Teaching American History,* William H. Cartwright and Richard L. Watson, Jr., co-editors. $4.00 (490-15838); cloth $5.00 (490-14840).

NATIONAL COUNCIL FOR THE SOCIAL STUDIES

1201 Sixteenth Street, N.W., Washington, D.C. 20036